Winning the HIRING GAME

Edward C. Andler

Smith Collins

Publishers & Consultants

Winning

The HIRI

IG GAME

Edward C. Andler

Editor: Gwyneth M. Vaughn

Cover & book designer: Curt Neitzke

Charts & graphs: Curt Neitzke

Manufacturing coordinator: O'Collins Corporation

Publisher's Cataloging in Publication Data

Andler, Edward C., 1932-
      Winning the Hiring Game / by Edward C. Andler.
         p.   cm.
      Includes bibliographical references (p.   ) and index.
      ISBN 0-9623414-2-8

      1. Employee selection. 2. Employment references.
      3. Personnel management. I. Title.
HF5549.5.S38A53   1992
658.3'112—dc20   91-66848

Printed in the United States of America

_To my late wife, Barbara, who
in spite of the disease which
eventually took her life was
closely involved in my work_

_Our daughter, Dara, who
provided tremendous personal
support and help during a very
challenging time in my life._

TABLE OF CONTENTS

INTRODUCTION

Background checking is the least used, but probably the single most productive phase in good hiring.

No management function is more critical than the hiring of people who will go on to become competent, motivated, and productive employees in your organization. That's why it is both ironic and surprising that the vast majority of hiring decisions are made without talking to the people who have actually observed a job applicant in action. In fact, most hiring decisions are based on how a small number of people "feel" about a particular job candidate after a few interviews.

This is not just an opinion, it is fact. It's a fact that most people are employed without even a cursory check with people who could provide valuable insight or confirmation about the applicants' past behavior or performance. It's a fact that most organizations and businesses are not adequately staffed to be able to take the necessary time to check candidates' backgrounds. And it's a fact that even in large corporations, a large percentage of jobs are filled without adequate reference checking by management or the personnel department.

Turnover Remains a Major Problem

Employee turnover would not be such a problem if the hiring practices of most companies today were effective, but such is not the case. Each year, American organizations spend an unbelievable amount of time, money, and energy on newly hired employees who do not work out and either leave on their own or are fired. In most instances, new employers have taken on previous employers' problems, a fact which now comes back to haunt them. Had the employer spent a little extra time and effort up front, and talked to the people who knew or worked with these applicants, far fewer bad hiring decisions would be made.

But the problem of ineffective hiring goes beyond the disturbingly high proportion of employees who either quit or are terminated after a relatively short time on the job. It extends to the millions of employees who do not leave but are marginal or mediocre workers who do only enough to get by. These marginal employees stay on the payroll but don't accomplish or produce nearly as much as well-fitted or highly motivated employees. They are costly burdens to the organization that hired them.

The problem is complicated even further by growing legal restraints on firing, which make it much more difficult to get rid of an employee for any reason without being sued. The litigation rate for some employers and in some geographic areas is rising rapidly. I once heard the vice president and chief legal officer of a large company, speaking at the company's annual human resource conference, say that he was greatly concerned because the largest number of his open cases—with probably the largest potential legal costs—involved "wrongful discharge" lawsuits. He went on to explain that, in his opinion, all of the discharge cases involved conduct and problems that should have been detected by good background checking when these persons were hired. He said, with a nod of agreement from the top human resource officer, that his company had to start doing a better job up front.

There Has to Be a Better Way

Based on my experience, I am convinced that the vast majority of hiring mistakes can be prevented by checking job candidates' past behavior, and this is not that hard to do. That's why I have written this book. My purpose can be explained simply: I want to help you ensure that you're hiring the people best suited for your job openings—and to avoid major hiring mistakes—through effective background reviews.

I hope to do this in two ways. *First,* I will help you to see why we are where we are on this matter of not checking out people. *Second,* I will show you what can be done to get background information easily and quickly.

This book was written to be used. It is not a book on personnel theory or legal interpretations. I firmly believe that most, if not all, of the training or explanations about employment screening have been confusing and even frightening, and, if anything, have made everyone more reluctant and impotent in this area. There is such a thing as bad training.

In this book, I focus on practical methods to help managers, supervisors, and professionals improve their ability to conduct background checks on prospective employees. Job seekers, too, may benefit from reading it, by better understanding the needs of hiring managers. The focus of this book is on technique, not theory; on action, not admonishment; on practical reasons, not psychological explanations as to why people do the things they do. In other words, I want to empower you to do a better job, not confuse you so you become less effective. My goal is to provide new and powerful ideas that will enable you to become immediately more proficient in this area. For most of you, it will probably be the first time you have heard what you can do in this regard. The book offers ways and means by which background checking can be improved.

Where I Come From

During my 25 years of nationwide staffing experience, I estimate that I have personally looked at more than 200,000 résumés and read about 30,000 of them, interviewed more than 6,000 people, and conducted more than 2,000 background checks on individual candidates, with more than 7,000 separate reference contacts. For the past six years, I have been on the service side of human resources as a major account representative and "headhunter" with the largest recruiting organization of its kind, most recently as a hiring consultant.

Since leaving corporate management, I have looked at the employment process as it is practiced in this country and wondered why we keep making the same mistakes. Fortunately, I have been able to stand back and get a much better view, and I can see that new thinking is definitely needed in this field. I am now devoting my time to applying new techniques to the process of background screening and evaluation for a diverse list of corporate clients. I have given special seminars on this subject throughout the United States. This training covers highly effective ways that can cut screening time in half—and double the results—whether carried out by staff or line employees. Hundreds of companies are now using these techniques.

If there is a single message to this book, it lies in this point: Put up your antennae and be open to fresh ideas. Review your present thinking and practices regarding hiring, then combine them with these new ideas—and you will greatly enhance your chances of choosing the right person for each job you fill. I truly believe that no organization in America will be successful in assembling a competitive work force in today's difficult times without turning to innovative, nontraditional strategies for selecting the best available workers.

Having pinpointed some of the most pressing problems, I have not been content to lament the decline of the employment game and let it go at that. I have attempted to give specific and positive solutions. Some are simple and practical; others are somewhat revolutionary. If they stimulate discussions and produce some healthy changes, I shall be happy. Change for the better is possible once everybody has enough information with which to work. I want to put common sense back into checking out candidates. So, let's be creative, "roll up our sleeves," and get to work to hire the right people for our organization.

The Background-Checking Formula

My whole philosophy on checking out candidates can be expressed with a short formula:

$$7W(LL) + IC + RT = SHD$$

By the time you finish, you'll know exactly what this formula means and how to make it work for you. In fact, you'll know so much about background screening, you'll probably invent a formula of your own.

Acknowledgments

Nothing great is possible without good friends and advisors.

I have had a great deal of help and advice from many people, including clients, participants in my seminars, and the thousands of references with whom I have spoken. Their views and comments helped me in developing new thinking and techniques on background checking. I would be remiss if I didn't acknowledge that many books and articles on this subject also spurred my thinking on the need to develop new concepts in this important yet often misunderstood phase of the employment process.

And there were these individuals who were especially helpful to me personally or played key roles in bringing this book together, including: Dara Andler-Herbst, my everyday assistant and advisor; Carol Eifert, my dear friend and companion; Gareth Gardiner, Ph.D., a great cheerleader and publisher; Linda Graves, a concerned typist; Curt Neitzke, who certainly knows layout and design; Dottie Niemayer, who is always ready to help; Linda Schaefer, a very conscientious typist and helper; Gwyneth Vaughn, an outstanding editor in every respect; Lois Vander Waerdt, J.D., who always gave me expert legal and business advice; and Edward Wilverding, a true friend and business associate.

Many thanks!

A Quiz

Before proceeding, let's see how much you know about checking out applicants. Answer the following questions with the first answer that comes to mind.

		Question
True	**False**	
❏	❏	1. About one out of ten job candidates will exaggerate or embellish his or her background.
❏	❏	2. Probably about 20 percent of executive applicants have their résumés written for them by someone else.
❏	❏	3. Attorneys who specialize in employment law advise against revealing information about a present or past employee.
❏	❏	4. The main reason for checking references is to see if a person is lying.
❏	❏	5. The references a candidate gives you aren't really very valuable because they are friends who are told what to say.
❏	❏	6. If someone is currently employed and you don't want to jeopardize his or her current job, there isn't much you can do to find out about him or her.
❏	❏	7. Asking a candidate to clarify unclear or confusing information that surfaced during your background checking is legally dangerous.
——	——	***Your Score***
T	**F**	

Now, let's examine each question.

Question No. 1: The latest surveys reflect that about one out of three job candidates will exaggerate or embellish his or her background. In fact, some recent studies show that figure to be higher. Enhancing one's work history is almost expected today.

Question No. 2: Probably about 75 percent of executive-level résumés have been written, or at least substantially rewritten, by someone else.

Question No. 3: Not all attorneys who specialize in employment law advise against revealing information about a present or past employee. Virtually every attorney recommends that an employer get as much information as possible before hiring someone. Progressive attorneys realize that it doesn't make sense to tell an employer to get relevant information from another employer, yet not to offer assistance when contacted by other employers—as long as it's done properly to minimize legal exposure.

Question No. 4: There are two reasons for checking references: (*a*) to see if the person is lying, but more importantly, (*b*) to determine the candidate's past job performance record and overall level of competence.

Question No. 5: Personal references provided by the candidate can be very valuable. They give you a place to start and can be used to get the names of other people who know the applicant. Also, with good questioning they will give you important insight into the person.

Question No. 6: If someone is currently employed and you don't want to jeopardize his or her job, there are always other people with whom you can speak. Individuals who recently left the company, clients or customers, co-workers close to the applicant who know what's going on, company retirees—all can serve as sources of information. Also, you would be surprised how often you have a current employee who used to work at the applicant's present company.

Question No. 7: Asking the candidate to clarify unclear or confusing information that surfaced during your background checking is really the fair thing to do. Put yourself in the candidate's shoes—isn't that what you would want?

So all the answers are false!

Hopefully, when you finish this book you will have no trouble agreeing with these explanations and conclusions. ☑

KNOW THE PROBLEM
Candidates Aren't Always What They Say They Are—in Many Ways

A WHOLE NEW GAME

Candidates have become very creative in presenting themselves.

The biggest problem in interviewing job candidates today is sorting out the truth from the fiction. Current surveys consistently indicate that at least one-third of all job seekers exaggerate—to some extent—their background and experience. In fact, some surveys have pegged the figure at 36 percent and even higher. The sales director of a large office-equipment dealer recently told me that he finds up to 50 percent of the people he interviews for sales positions mislead him in some way.

Suffice it to say that a high number of job seekers today are willing to modify who they are, what they can do, or what they have done in order to find new employment. If you haven't been checking out your employees before you hire them, you can figure that possibly a third of the people working for you gained their jobs by creatively presenting their background and capabilities to your hiring "experts." And, this probably happens in good times when there are plenty of jobs to go around. When the job market tightens, of course, there is even more reason to distort the facts.

My firm, Certified Reference Checking Company, spent a number of weeks researching résumé distortion. The amount of misrepresentation reported by reliable surveys in past years clearly indicates that the problem has been rising steadily over the years. In 1991 misrepresentation was reported to be approximately 36 percent; in 1981 it was about 23 percent; whereas in 1977 it was only 17 percent. This can be seen clearly in Figure 1-1. We did not go further back than 1977, but I can recall that back in the mid-1960s, the figure spoken of was in the 10 percent range.

Clearly, there is measurable evidence that dishonesty is now a very significant factor which must be dealt with in today's employment scene. There is a growing realization that job market lying has gone too far.

Our Changing Society

Most people agree that Americans are less ethical than in the past. Is it because honesty is no longer cherished, or that we don't know right from wrong any more? In the 1980s the newspapers and evening news were filled with stories of ethical breakdown. Scientists were caught faking their findings; defense contractors were indicted for bribery; prominent Wall Street brokers were jailed for insider trading; religious leaders were exposed for sleeping around. Congress had difficulty deciding what ethical standards apply to its members, while the tremendous drain on the taxpayers from the savings and loan debacle will haunt us for years.

This trend is showing up throughout society. Employee theft and shoplifting have created a significant increase in retail shrinkage over the past decade. And theft losses keep rising despite retailers' increased investment in security systems to protect themselves. Many use a two-tag system—a visible hard tag and an invisible secondary device—to deter thieves. More stores are filing charges against shoplifters, often using videotaped evidence to get convictions. Even modern pay phones have been modified for today's world with such antivandalism features as steel-coated cords, one-piece receivers, and "no-pick" locks.

Figure 1-1

Résumé Distortion

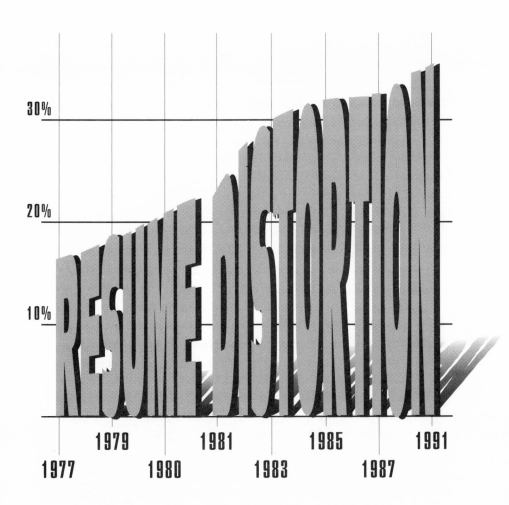

Source: Certified Reference Checking Company

The point is that we have a serious dishonesty problem at practically all levels of society, and we are responding to it. Personally, we are placing security devices on our own homes and automobiles to protect our most prized possessions. New methods and equipment are coming on the market every day to safeguard ourselves and our property. Security has become big business.

The Ostrich Approach

On the other hand, in the area of employment screening, where we know and recognize that there is also a very serious problem, little—and in most cases, nothing—is being done to protect employers. The legal community and human resource professionals have essentially thrown up their hands and taken the position that there just isn't much that can be done about job applicants' dishonesty. The very people who are supposed to spot dishonesty by job seekers have allowed—almost encouraged—this to happen. We all know this to be true from the few calls that we receive from other employers requesting information about our former employees. The result is a vicious form of recycling: Employers are simply recycling the marginal or poor performers among themselves.

I call this the "ostrich approach" to the major problem in hiring—dishonesty by job applicants. Like the ostrich, we hide our heads in the sand and try to avoid the danger by refusing to face it. In the process, we have removed the major reason for being honest when applying for employment.

When we do not check out the information job applicants tell us, we provide an opportunity for questionable individuals to take advantage of the situation and lie to us. Eventually, even the honest job seekers will resort to falsification just to keep up with the dishonest ones who are getting by on false pretenses.

As the employment director of a large banking institution in a major city told me: "In the banking business in our town, we are all keeping our best tellers. What we are doing, however, is exchanging the poor ones among ourselves. I want to get out of this loop." When you stop to think about it, it doesn't make much sense to fire a poor employee and then turn right around and hire another bad employee. Yet when you fail to take the time to check out those you hire, that's exactly what you are doing. If you hire someone else's problem, you're right back where you started. That's precisely why many companies are never able to upgrade their work force.

In my business of providing third-party reference-checking services for client companies throughout the country, we have found that about 15 percent of the job candidates we check out do not get hired because of the information we uncover. Just think how nice it would be to be able to spot these individuals yourself and not bring them on board.

In my reference-checking practice, I have found that when I report to an employer that a candidate has falsified his or her background in some way, the employer is glad to have discovered the discrepancy in advance of offering the person employment. I frequently hear comments like, "They just never learn they can't get by lying to us." The problem is that job seekers have learned they can lie and probably get by with it—most of the time. This just happened to be a rare case where someone was caught.

Stretching the Truth

To see how distortion occurs in the job market, let's look at the case of a sales candidate (let's call him Fred) who, over the last ten years, has been a typical average performer with his current employer. At year-end, Fred has consistently been in the middle among the 20-member company sales force. Some years he was a little above average; other years he was slightly below the middle mark. Now, like most sales people, there have been some very good months when Fred was near the top in sales . He has also won some special sales contests, and opened a number of good accounts. Over the long haul, though, the middle has been his place among the group. He is a reliable, but not exceptional sales employee. Fred knows this and his current employer is well aware of his predictable level of performance.

Fred has now decided to look for new employment, and he can present his previous employment record in a number of ways. Obviously, he can be very straightforward and honest and tell it like it is. But, let's say he decides to "fluff" his background somewhat as he goes out for interviews.

Fred tells a prospective new employer that he was one of his company's best salesmen. Now this is not really false, because there were times when he was near the top. In other words, he has conveniently exaggerated his past performance in a way that makes him look good. This is probably a fairly normal occurrence.

But now, let's say Fred tells an employer that he was so competent that he was singled out to train other sales representatives. The fact of the matter is that the entire sales force was brought in every Friday from 7:00 A.M. to 9:00 A.M. for refresher training, and each sales representative was assigned various subjects on a routine basis to cover for about an hour. Fred, like all the other members of the sales group, was periodically given a topic to cover. He was not singled out for his expertise as he would like the potential employer to believe, but was merely used as a trainer at times as a way to fulfill the training need. Fred has deliberately misrepresented his role in order to get the new employer to think that he was so good he was personally selected to train the other salespeople, which in fact is not really the case at all. I believe you would agree that this is a much more serious distortion of the facts.

Now let's say Fred tells a potential employer that he was in the top 10 percent of his company's sales force last year—an outright lie. I believe all of us would consider this to be a clear and obvious attempt to get us to believe he is something he is not.

If you discovered the truth—which you can do—you will probably react in a fairly predictable way. In the first case of exaggeration, you may still hire Fred, depending on how everything else looks. In the second instance, where there was obvious misrepresentation, you would most likely lose interest in him as a candidate. And, in the third situation, where Fred lied to you, you would definitely call it off.

The Bottom Line

Bad news usually costs a lot less if you get it sooner rather than later. What is the real effect of exaggeration, misrepresentation, and lying by job candidates? Like buying a product or service that's not what it's advertised to be, you're not getting what you think you're getting. The lesson to be learned is probably best summed up in an old gambler's proverb: "Always trust your fellow man—and always cut the cards." Or, to use a more modern version relating to arms-reduction proposals:

TRUST BUT VERIFY

The bottom line is that repeated surveys point that out at least one out of three job applicants does not tell the whole truth. There is no law or requirement that job applicants have to tell you their flaws or even be truthful. It is the employer's task to find the distortions or lies.

Someone with a past alcohol problem once asked me if he should bring it up during an upcoming job interview. I suggested that he might not want to volunteer the information; however, if it came up, he should be very honest, straightforward, and willing to explain where he is at this time in his recovery program.

It's time for Real World 101. Our hiring practices must be based on reality, not wishful thinking. The airline industry faced the problem of hijacking a number of years ago and now carefully checks all luggage. It's time for employers to face their problem and start checking who they are bringing on board.

Change can creep up on us and we don't even realize it's happening. It's a new age with new challenges for businesses to face and solve. For those of you who are your company's "gatekeepers," with the responsibility to keep the wrong people from being hired, there has to be a way to solve this problem. Fortunately, there are creative measures that can be taken, as we will show you throughout this book. ☑

THE CANDIDATE'S ADVANTAGE

The scale now dips toward the applicant.

The current job market has bred an increasingly savvy crop of applicants. In fact, the whole employment process has shifted in favor of job seekers. Motivated job seekers can draw from innumerable services, specialists, and products to hone their interviewing skills. There literally is a whole industry out there to help job seekers—including career counseling or outplacement assistance, professional résumé writers, search firms and employment agencies, to say nothing of the numerous books, and audio- and videotapes on how to find a job, and even computer programs to track them through their entire job search. Let's look closer at each of those and see how they can help and, in many cases, really "polish up" an applicant.

Career Counseling and Outplacement

Career counseling has been around a long time. Most of us probably used career counselors in high school or college. Frequently,

11

counselors are teachers who may not really know or be experienced in the business world. If reasonably competent, however, counselors can help point job seekers in the right direction.

Outplacement comes in two forms: retail and company-paid. You have probably seen advertisements for retail career-planning firms* in big city newspapers and phone books. Many firms have come and gone in this arena—some with dubious reputations for professional conduct and results. These firms cater to those who are looking for jobs or want to make a career change. They emphasize their career marketing services for moving candidates through the job market using planning and personal assistance programs. They try to find candidates who are finding their job search too time consuming or unproductive—and charge a substantial fee to help them.

Company-paid outplacement firms are retained by corporations to help terminated employees land new jobs. They start out by trying to minimize the trauma associated with termination and then develop a structured program to guide employees in their job search. They usually prepare résumés and give personalized attention to each individual with follow-up guidance as needed. Their goal is to reduce the time necessary to locate a new position. Their fees, which vary depending on the level of service provided, are based on a pre-arranged understanding with the last employer.

Both retail and company-paid services basically follow a similar outline that involves explaining the realities of the job market, writing an effective résumé, developing techniques to generate interviews, targeting industries and organizations, and helping with letter-writing campaigns. Many also provide interview training with actual practice on videotape. Obviously, a good firm can be a tremendous help to job candidates in understanding and tackling the tough business of finding the right new job.

---

* Also referred to at times as career-management, career-development, or career-transition firms.

Résumé-Preparation Services

A résumé says basically: Here's where I have worked, here's what I did, and here's how good I was at it. A whole industry has been built around the preparation and production of the mythical "perfect" résumé.

Résumé-writing services and help now abound everywhere—both formally and informally. A high percentage of résumés are either entirely written or at least rewritten for job hunters. At one time, the résumé basically indicated a candidate's writing ability and knowledge of grammar. That's not the case anymore. The higher the job level, the greater is the chance a résumé was prepared professionally. At the executive level, almost all résumés have a professional touch.

Experts in the employment field advise that the primary purpose of a résumé is to get an interview. After all, a résumé initially gets examined for about 20 seconds and then a decision is made whether or not to interview the candidate. It is in the interview that the candidate must sell himself (or herself) to get a job. The résumé should therefore be succinct and to the point—like a good product advertisement. It should contain just enough information to convince the employer to call the person for an interview. Unfortunately, many candidates don't realize this and create long and rambling documents that are actually boring and self-defeating. A candidate is ahead of the competition if the résumé does nothing to unsell his or her candidacy.

You might ask, so what if a résumé is puffed up a little bit? Perhaps you believe that it's all right if the résumé attempts to present the candidate in the best light. The problem is that the résumé is the candidate's script, and if it is exaggerated or falsified, that message has to be carried out through the entire hiring process.

Job-Hunting Books, Tapes, and Computer Programs

There are a lot of books, audiotapes, and videotapes on the market about how to do well and be successful in finding new employment.

Most of them are good and offer sound advice to the perplexed, confused, or even desperate job seeker. Goodness knows, looking for a job is a rough situation for most people and even frightening for many. Therefore, any help or encouragement they can get is desirable and needed.

More and more, today's emphasis is on the use of computers and on-line databases that match job seekers to positions, recruiters to job seekers, or allow an individual to scan openings that may be of interest. There are a variety of computerized databases that allow applicants the opportunity to research companies or industries quickly and comprehensively according to size, revenues, product, location, or any other meaningful combination. Such comprehensive resources provide ready information to job seekers and reduce the amount of time spent researching target companies and trying to figure out what they want. It is now possible to pinpoint through database resources companies to which to send your résumé. Thus, more time and attention can actually be spent on trying to capture the position sought, and this further tips the whole process toward the applicant.

Search Firms and Employment Agencies

Talking about the advantage candidates have in the job market wouldn't be complete without mentioning the way search firms and employment agencies go out of their way to help candidates. Let's face it, search firms and agencies have one purpose—to place people in new jobs and get paid for doing it. Although these services may extol their desire to match the right people to the right job, the bottom line is that they have to place people to pay their bills and stay in business (which a lot of them don't).

The first step these firms take is to identify their candidate's strong points and then sell prospective employers on seeing their candidate. They usually do a better job than a job hunter would have done on his or her own behalf, because most of us aren't that comfortable bragging about ourselves. They then prepare the person for the interview by telling him what the company, the job, and the interviewers are like.

14

They will sometimes go into great detail on what questions to anticipate and how to answer them. They may even advise the candidate on the idiosyncrasies and preferences of the company's interviewers, so the candidate will be better prepared to handle them or even take control over them. An employment consultant at one of the nation's largest placement firms told me: "I may spend up to two hours coaching my candidate on how to beat the interview and win the job. I want him to be the one who's selected. That's how I earn my living."

I have seen written summaries from employment firms that were really "cooked"—that is, they omitted important and unfavorable items of information, or so cleverly disguised negative points that they didn't appear to be the problem they really were. In fact, I have even seen cases where dates of employment have been moved around to make a candidate look like she had a record of being continuously employed during her career—which she wasn't.

A Candidate's Appearance

The candidate who stands before an interviewer is at his or her very best. He or she probably has on a new suit or dress, has cleaned and spruced up, and is making a real effort to be a pleasant and likable human being. We have all had to look for a job and know that this is what to do. We want to put our best foot forward. Someone who smokes, for example, knows almost instinctively not to light up a cigarette during an interview, even though he is an inveterate smoker who normally can't go 15 minutes without smoking.

A client once told me about a receptionist she hired who completely fooled her. The company, which is housed in a beautiful building with very modern and impressive offices, is an elite firm and wanted to project that image quickly to visitors. The manager twice interviewed one young lady who seemed to have it all. She was pretty, well dressed, and well spoken. She looked like a perfect fit for the reception desk in the company's exclusive surroundings. But when she came to work the first day, the staff could hardly believe their eyes. Her hair and make-up were almost outlandish, her clothes were too trendy, and her speech and actions were completely different from what she had projected in the interviews. The personnel specialist and the manager responsible for hiring her immediately went into conference on what to do. When the company chairman came through the reception area and did a "double take," he immediately sought out those responsible for hiring this immature young girl for such a visible position.

To make a long story short, she had borrowed both outfits she wore when interviewed; a friend had helped her with her make-up and hair to get a more businesslike image; and she even had some special coaching on how to speak and act in a mature manner. She portrayed the role very well and got the job, but in fact she was a very young girl who didn't have a business wardrobe, and really didn't want to conform to fit in a professional environment. It was all a facade.

This happens every day. It's the way the game is played. Men are told to shave off their beards if they have one (grow it back after being hired), get a haircut, wear a conservative suit, shine their shoes, and other appropriate advice. Women are told to adopt a businesslike appearance and demeanor, and other pertinent advice suitable to the level and type of position for which they are applying.

What it all comes down to is that what you see and hear when you interview someone is not always what you get in the long run. The whole hiring situation has often become a big game of fooling the interviewer. Thankfully, you can find out what the person is really like if you take the time and effort to go back and talk to the people who have known or worked with the applicant in the past. The information is there if *you will seek it out* as we will see later.☑

IT'S TIME TO REGAIN CONTROL

The minute the employer loses control of the hiring process, the advantage goes to the applicant.

There are two basic reasons job candidates lie:

❑ *To avoid something that will lower their standing in the interviewer's eyes (in order not to lose out to the other applicants)*

❑ *To appear more competent and valuable to the firm (that is, create a higher compensation need)*

Candidates know instinctively that they are competing against other job seekers for a particular job. Depending on the position and the number of people willing to fill it, there is competition. The person chosen will somehow have to win over everyone else. Coming in second is like coming in last. It's serious business and we all know this. So for many applicants, being successful means bending the facts to be the victor.

How much a person is worth is a subjective decision made by the employer. Where a candidate fits in a job or salary range—top, middle, or bottom—is based on someone's evaluation of the candidate's experience and competency. For a new employee, this judgment has to be made using the information provided by the candidate and anyone else the employer chooses to contact.

The situation is further complicated by the fact that companies usually pay new employees based on how much it takes to get them to go to work for the new employer, not necessarily how much they are worth. If, for whatever reason, the candidate is low paid in his or her present job, you can almost bet the new employer will offer a comparably low salary. Conversely, if the person is paid on the high side (even if this is not fully deserved), the new employer will offer a similarly high salary. In effect, employers have brought about this problem of salary inflation by candidates simply because employers are so influenced by it. This practice of allowing previous salary to dictate the new salary may help explain why minorities and women are often paid less than their white male counterparts.

We all know how the game is played because we have played it ourselves. You were probably brought into your present position and paid based largely on how much you were making at your previous company. The name of the game is for the candidate to think of salary in the highest possible terms, and, of course, to try to convey a high compensation need to a future employer.

In one of my seminars, a lady told a story about her husband's actual experience in the job market. Early in his career he interviewed for a new job and was asked what his current annual salary was. He replied, "20-8," meaning $20,800. He saw the interviewer write it down and thought nothing more of it. When he was offered the position at $29,500 he was astonished. Apparently, the interviewer wrote down $28,000 and then made an offer using that figure as a guide. The woman swore the story was true, commenting that it really made a difference in their income level over the years—making that big one-time jump in pay at a critical time. Table 3-1 shows other things that job seekers may do to win a job.

Table 3-1

How/Why Applicants Misrepresent Themselves

Educational Background
- List degree(s) never attained—to appear well educated.
- List school(s) not attended—for prestige value.
- Include outside course work never started/completed—to appear industrious.
- Make up participation in campus activites—to appear well rounded.

Employment History
- Stretch dates of employment—to cover periods of unemployment.
- Omit certain employers—to hide unsatisfactory employment.
- List company that is out of business or has been absorbed—to make checking difficult or impossible.

Salary and Job Title
- Inflate previous salary—to create higher compensation need.
- Embellish job title—to appear more successful.

Expertise and Achievements
- Indicate supervisory/management roles not held—to reflect leadership ability.
- Embellish duties and responsibilities—to appear more experienced and successful.
- Indicate performance levels not attained—to appear more competent.
- Exaggerate results achieved (sales, profits, programs)—to appear more successful.

Self-Employment
- List self-employment or personal consulting—to cover a period of unemployment or a job that didn't work out.
- Exaggerate self-employed accomplishments—to appear successful.

Criminal Record
- Omit convictions—to remove any doubt regarding honesty or reliability.
- Downplay past record—to divert attention from personal problems.

References
- List well-known or important people—to impress employer.
- Program references to say the right things—to cover misrepresentation.

Source: Certified Reference Checking Company

To put it simply, there are real-world reasons for altering the facts or even lying when looking for a job. In the area of education, for example, surveys repeatedly show that a college degree greatly increases earning power. In comparing the median income of college-educated men and women and high-school-educated men and women, college graduates receive about a third more income. Is it any mystery why someone who didn't finish (or even attend) college will show a degree on her résumé—especially when she doesn't think it will ever be checked?

The 'X' Factor

What has happened in the job market can best be seen by examining the "X" Factor, shown in Figure 3-1. The "X" Factor is simply two lines. The control line represents the amount of checking by the employer; the reaction line is the amount of lying by applicants. What it shows is that as the amount of checking decreases, the amount of lying increases.

For whatever reason—probably legal interpretations and equal employment considerations—the amount of reference checking by employers throughout the United States has been steadily declining. Those candidates who are inclined to be dishonest have sensed this and taken advantage of it. The problem is that candidates who would prefer to be honest in presenting themselves know that unless they too embellish who they are, they may get left behind. The whole situation has resulted in a serious and increasing mess in today's job market.

Now let's look at how this phenomenon affects individual companies. You can bet that if your company has let slip the amount of background verification it does, people in the job market are probably aware of it—and are taking advantage of the situation. Word gets out quickly as to where you can go and say what you want and get by with it, and where you can't.

I tell people who attend my seminars on employment screening that while they are sleeping, applicants are thinking up ways to fool them. I relay a story that actually happened to me many years ago when

Figure 3-1

The 'X' Factor

HIGH

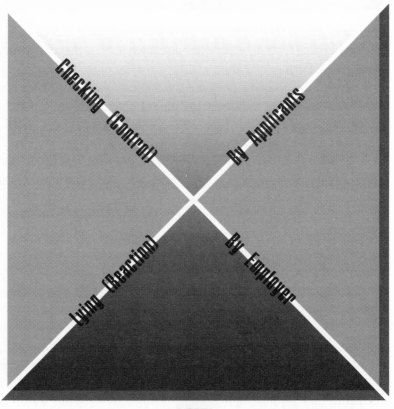

LOW

Source: Certified Reference Checking Company

I was a personnel manager at a large manufacturing plant in the Los Angeles area. We had an employee working in the plant who seriously hurt his back doing heavy lifting. After I took him to the company doctor for x-rays, the doctor told me this employee—who had been with us about three months—had really hurt himself. He also advised that the employee had a deformed back and should not be working for us, much less doing heavy lifting. I reminded the doctor that he had given this person a pre-employment physical, which included a back x-ray, and he hadn't told us not to hire him at that time. He said, "Oh-oh," and started comparing medical records. It turned out that the employee had someone else (25 pounds heavier and 5 inches taller) take his physical for him, yet no one had caught it. To make a long story short, we immediately started a companywide procedure requiring applicants to sign a health questionnaire at the employment office and then countersign it at the doctor's office. Using driver's licenses to compare the signature and photograph is another good way to double check who you are actually working with.

Candidates can be smart and clever people who can thwart the employment process in strange and alarming ways. Unfortunately, too many dishonest candidates are taking advantage of the system, and even the honest ones are forced to be devious to keep up with them.

Pre-Employment Considerations

The need to check out those we are hiring has never been greater. There are three basic problem candidates employers need to be able to spot:

1. *Those who are underqualified*–Those who simply don't have the background, knowledge, or skills to be able to function in today's complex job categories.
2. *Those who are burned out*–Many job seekers have just stayed in something too long and are tired and worn out. They need to get out of their old line of work and get into something new.

3. *Those who are emotionally unstable*–The number of people with serious and continuing emotional problems is a national concern. Alcoholism and drug dependency have become a widespread problem and spawned a whole new rehabilitation industry.

The problem is that most candidates don't see or try to see that they are underqualified, burned out, or no longer emotionally fit for the type of work they are doing. Even if there have been troubles in their careers that clearly point out that they may not be well suited to their work, they continue to seek out jobs in the same line of work.

A couple of actual cases come to mind:

A credit manager in a large manufacturing company was fired for general indifference and lack of interest in his work. He had started out many years before as a credit analyst and progressed upward into credit management. He really didn't enjoy processing requests for credit and the large amount of administration connected with it, and it was obvious that he was just hanging on for the generous benefits and retirement the company offered. The company saw his bad attitude and low level of performance and asked him to leave. What kind of new position did he look for? You guessed it—credit management.

A sales manager had been an outstanding sales representative prior to being promoted into sales management. However, he had lost his zip and interest and didn't do well in everyday sales administration. He had developed a bad drinking problem that was beginning to affect his health, family, and general well being. He was let go and was on the job market looking for employment as—you guessed it— a sales manager.

A hiring mismatch is harmful in many ways. It takes a heavy psychic toll in stress and unhappiness on the individual, which can be transmitted to his or her family—and even to a pet, which may be mistreated. Certainly, other employees notice and feel the impact of someone who is not up to or doing his or her job. In fact, they are the first to notice and to be affected by substandard job performance. And finally, an employer's business image, productivity, and even profits can be damaged or seriously reduced by employees not able or willing to do their jobs properly.

Let's end this discussion on a humorous note. Even the best of us doesn't always tell the truth all the time. The story goes that a minister told his congregation that the following week he would preach on lying. He asked them to read the 17th chapter of the Gospel of St. Mark in the meantime. The next Sunday he asked how many had done the reading he had assigned. Several hands went up. "I see," said the minister. "You are the very people I want to reach. There is no 17th chapter in St. Mark's Gospel."

The Honesty/Competency Scale

Whether we realize it or not, we are consciously or subconsciously trying to determine *two* factors when we screen job candidates. We want to find out how honest they are being with us, and how competent they are on the job. Figure 3-2, the "Honesty/Competency Scale," is always a real eye-opener to those I present it to in my public and private seminars on employment screening.

A candidate would always like for us to believe that he is the ideal person for the job opening, that he is being totally honest, and that he is a top performer in his field. Many of us know from Psychology 101 in college that people fall along a "bell curve" in all aspects of their personality or other characteristics. There are a few people at the extreme ends of the curve, which means they are either very good or very poor in that attribute. However, the vast majority fall into that great middle group who are above average, average, or below average. Therefore, among a group of candidates interviewed for a position, each person will fall somewhere along a spectrum of talents and abilities.

Figure 3-2

The Honesty/Competency Scale

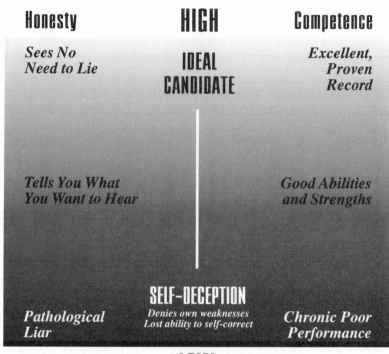

Honesty	HIGH	Competence
Sees No Need to Lie	**IDEAL CANDIDATE**	*Excellent, Proven Record*
Tells You What You Want to Hear		*Good Abilities and Strengths*
Pathological Liar	**SELF-DECEPTION** *Denies own weaknesses Lost ability to self-correct*	*Chronic Poor Performance*

LOW

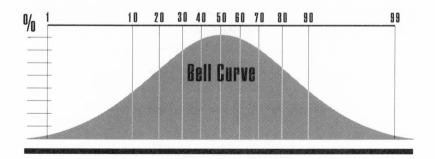

Bell Curve

Let's look at the Honesty Scale in Figure 3-2. There are applicants who see no need to be anything but totally honest. The vast majority, however, will generally tell you what you want to hear. If you are interviewing a programmer and you ask her if she has ever been involved in payroll programming, chances are she will quickly recall a situation where she did get involved in this area of computerization—telling you what you have signaled you want to hear. Or, let's take a more personal situation. Let's say you are somewhat concerned about whom your teenage son is associating with, and ask, "Are those good boys you are spending your time around?" Picking up on your clue, he will probably answer, "Sure, they are. Why, Billie's dad is a minister, and Joey's dad is a doctor," replying with what he knows you want to hear. He took your cue and gave you the reassurance you wanted.

On the Competency Scale of Figure 3-2, there are a few people who are top and proven performers. Then there are those who are chronically poor performers, sometimes not even realizing they are at that low level; most people, however, will fall into the generally average category of performance. No matter what the job level or category—executives, technicians, or streetsweepers—there are top performers, average performers, and low performers. When presidents of the United States leave office, what do they worry about? They wonder if they will go down in history as great presidents, average ones, or poor ones.

There are top performers in every area or occupation. I remember reading about the top bulldozer operator in the country as determined in the annual National Truck and Equipment Rodeo competition. Friends of mine who are airline pilots tell me that they can sit next to another pilot with whom they have never flown and, in minutes, are able to tell how good a pilot the other one is. Think of this scale even for the carpenter who is going to build a porch for your house. Checking out how good someone is can apply to many areas of our lives, even outside the workplace.

Management's View

I speak with executives, managers, and staff members in organizations throughout the country on the subject of background reviews, and I ask them to what extent they check the references of prospective employees who are applying for jobs with their company. The answer from top management is invariably that they are always checked, or checked most of the time. When I talk to middle managers—who are closer to what's actually going on, they advise that the references of their job candidates get checked about 75 percent of the time. However, when I review the subject with the staff personnel actually responsible for doing the checking, they will honestly admit that references get checked in only about 50 to 60 percent of the cases, and even then it's not always done very thoroughly.

The point is that management knows that the background of those hired by the company should be checked. It's just good business sense. The problem is that when it goes down to the level where it has to be done, it's a different story. The whole process of checking out job applicants gets shortchanged or is not done at all.

The problem, as we will see in this book, is that it is too burdensome to check references the way we have been led to believe it has to be done. There just isn't enough time or people to chase down references in today's companies where the hiring staffs are leaner and busier than they have ever been before.

Panning for Gold

Pyrite, a mineral which is light yellow with a metallic luster, was often mistaken for real gold during the gold rush years. It fooled enough prospectors to inspire its nickname "fool's gold." To be sure of what they had, the prospectors would have it assayed.

Unfortunately, many interviewers have been similarly fooled by job candidates who gave the appearance and impression of being the real thing. However, under close examination through background checking, they turned out not to be so exceptional. Some applicants tell you who and what they would like to be rather than who and what they really are. Don't assume that someone is even marginally competent, no matter how good he or she claims to be. Make the candidate prove it through verified job performance. If he or she can't prove it, pass.

My advice to companies is to make checking references the last hurdle in the employment process. In other words, go through the full evaluation process and then check references to be sure that what you have been led to believe is, in fact, true and correct. Some employers will get down to the last few candidates and then contact references to obtain information upon which to base a final selection decision. I never recommend this as an effective way to use reference checking because it places too much emphasis on what the references have to say; but mainly because it strains the whole system through the heavy workload it creates.

Checking the background of job candidates has never been more important. On the other hand, due to reorganizations and downsizings, most companies and the people who do employment screening have less time than ever to devote to the task. They are already overworked, and consequently this function often gets neglected. We are into a new era which requires new thinking and actions to get back on track.

Avoid the Problem Altogether

You can avoid hiring totally unknown people by being your own recruiter. There is nothing that prevents an organization from going out on its own and recruiting proven, top performers that it knows about. Most line or staff managers belong to associations or have some contact with other people in their specialty or career field. They have met or at least heard about individuals with excellent reputations. If you're looking for a state tax supervisor, for example, think of those with a top standing in this field. Call these people and let them know you have a position opening. If they are interested, have them come in; at least ask them to think about it and call you back if they would like to pursue the opportunity. Any employment specialist worth his salt will always ask the manager with an opening if he or she knows of anyone in particular who would fit in the job. Then you can start your search with these candidates. If you turn an opening over to an outside recruiting firm, they will often ask if there are any individuals—by name—you would really like to interview. They will then contact those persons and, if possible, feed them back to you. Why not avoid the expense and do it yourself? If it bothers you to make this contact as a representative of your company, hire someone to do it at a fraction of what you would have to pay to have these people eventually sent to you as a result of an expensive outside search effort.

If you are looking for a job and hear that a certain company which you would like to work for has an opening, contact that company and let them know of your interest before they have to start an expensive and time-consuming recruiting effort. You may find that you have practically clear sailing into the job. Why wait for the opening to appear in the newspaper, when you then become just one of the many unknown respondents with whom a company has to deal?

Due to the difficulty of trying to screen job candidates today, a rapidly growing trend among organizations is to use temporary employees who can be cut loose if they aren't suitable or are not working out well on the job. A company can then hire permanent employees from this pool of people, after observing them over a period of time. In industry this is now jokingly referred to as a "try and buy" or "rent to hire" program.

A little initiative by both the employer and the candidate can go a long way toward helping to solve the dilemma of the unknown applicant who has to be carefully screened and checked out to avoid unexpected future surprises after he goes to work.☑

A survey conducted by Certified Reference Checking Company revealed that 34 percent of job applicants embellished, misrepresented, or even lied about their backgrounds when presenting themselves for a job.

The study was based on over 1,200 confidential background checks conducted during 1991, 1990, and 1989. These conclusions were based on feedback given by references during a thorough review of the background of candidates. Surprisingly, there was not any significant difference in data among executive, professional, administrative, or production candidates.

Some applicants misrepresented themselves in more than one category, such as exaggerating achievements, and then lying about salary. But overall, the study found that today's job applicants misrepresent themselves as follows: 22 percent, expertise and achievements; 12 percent, salary and job title; 11 percent, employment history; 9 percent, educational background; 4 percent, self-employment; 3.5 percent, criminal record; and 1.5 percent, false references.

WRAPPING IT UP

What we know . . . but don't see about the growing problem of dishonesty today.

❏ If we don't check out what people tell us, many questionable individuals will take advantage of the situation and *lie* to us.

❏ Eventually, even *honest* people will resort to falsification in order to keep up with the dishonest ones who are getting by on false pretenses.

❏ We live in a world where even our top political and business leaders openly lie and cheat and suffer *no* consequences for their behavior—setting a terrible example for all to follow.

And in conclusion . . .

❏ All these factors come into play with the increasing dishonesty in the job market today, and therefore–*now more than ever!*–we need to be diligent and check out what we're told by applicants.

LEGAL AND REGULATORY LIMITS
Employers—Both Former and Prospective—Have the Right to Discuss an Applicant's Past Performance

5 LEGAL QUESTIONS

The applicant's basic civil rights must never be violated.

I have noticed that hiring professionals look at the legal issues of screening job candidates from two different perspectives. The first group clearly wants to check all applicants' backgrounds to ensure that everything is all right, and they want to be sure they are doing it legally. The second group wants to learn about and be conversant on the legal reasons why it is not advisable to check up on people, because deep down they just don't want to do it. They become part of the problem, instead of part of the solution.

I warn you in advance that those in the first group will be very pleased with this discussion, whereas the second group will be sorely disappointed. We are going to take a look at what legally *can be done,* not what *can't be done,* in getting information about a job candidate's past actions and performance.

Let's first look at this matter from a historical perspective. There was a time, not long ago, when the "best jobs" were filled primarily by white men. Then, due to long overdue governmental and societal pressures, employers were forced to interview and consider women and minority group members for all job openings. To be fair and not discriminate against anyone, federal and state governments passed laws and regulations to assure that everyone is treated equally and fairly when seeking employment.

Let's look at it this way. We all know we literally have to "jump hurdles" to get a new job with a company; this is commonly referred to as going through the employment process. Now, if a white male has three hurdles; a white female, four hurdles; a minority male, five hurdles; and a minority female, six hurdles, this would hardly be fair— at least for those with the extra hurdles. Everyone should be subject to the same terms and rules when being considered for employment. That's just being fair!

Ask the Right Questions

Many hours and dollars have been spent trying to train hiring officials as to what questions they can legally ask of job applicants and their references. From my experience, this training is usually presented in a very legalistic and complicated manner that ends up confusing those doing the hiring; in the end, it just makes them more frightened and less effective at checking out job candidates. I believe that you can boil it all down to these *two* basic rules which will keep you out of trouble 99 and 44/100 percent of the time.

❏ *Ask* all *applicants the same questions. Don't direct different questions to different groups (women, minority members, handicapped).*

❏ All *questions must be job related. Do not ask for personal information.*

Play it safe. Stay with questions that have to do with education, training, work history, and job-related skills.

Using a typical case, let's look at what we mean by asking all applicants the same questions. Suppose you are interviewing a young mother who has two young children for a marketing position. Can you ask her how she is going to take care of these children while she is working? No, because you wouldn't ask a man this question, and additionally, it is not related to her ability to perform her work. You can, however, define the job conditions for her, explaining that she may periodically have to work overtime on short notice, or that she will be expected to work one Saturday a month. Then, with this background, you can ask her if your job fits and meets her personal and family needs. Exactly what her child care arrangements are is none of your concern.

Or, let's take the case of a young minority factory applicant who, as you noticed from your office window, drives an old dilapidated automobile. Can you ask him during the employment interview if his car will be able to get him back and forth to work? Again, the answer is no, because you wouldn't ask the same question of another applicant (who may be driving his father's new car), and the question is not related to his ability to do the job. Again, however, you can define the hours and conditions of work, which, let's say are 7:00 A.M. to 4:00 P.M., with the need to work overtime as needed. You might also explain that the local bus which goes by the plant operates only from 6:00 A.M. to 6:00 P.M. With this background, you can then ask the young man if he will be able to get to work on time and get home at the end of his shift. How he will do this is his problem and should not concern you.

The point is that you cannot create "extra hurdles" for some candidates, over those that are already laid out for other applicants. Your questions must be related to the job, which, when you really stop to think about it, is the only fair way to treat job applicants.

Now that you have this background, look at the Table 5-1, which shows what you can and cannot ask in certain areas. Also, these interpretations on legal questions will apply to what you can ask when checking references, as we will see later in Chapter 15.

Table 5-1

Legal Inquiries Before Hiring

Under federal law, there can be no job discrimination based on sex, race color, religion, national origin, or age. Consequently, there are topics you should not ask a prospective employee because they may be discriminatory.

Item	You Can Ask	You Cannot ask
Age	Whether candidate is above minimum or maximum age	Age, birth date, birth certificate, high school graduation date
Criminal Record	Conviction record, if it relates to ability to do the job	Arrest record
Credit Rating	Anything that directly relates to ability to do the job	Anything that does not relate to ability to do the job
Disabilities	Anything that directly relates to ability to do the job	Anything that does not relate to ability to do the job
Work Schedule	Willingness to work required work schedule	Willingness to work any particular religious holiday
Marital/Family Status	Nothing	Anything
Military Record	Type of experience related to the job	Military service in any other country
National Origin	Whether candidate can legally work in the U.S.	Anything
Race, Religion, Sex	Nothing	Anything

Source: Certified Reference Checking Company

Employment Discrimination

There is a very fundamental concept in employment that must be honored: The nature of the questions you ask cannot reduce the chances of minorities or women being hired. You must be able to show that the responses to any questions asked are not used to eliminate any member of a protected class from consideration. In other words, if the answer you get becomes a factor in your decision, and it will eliminate a member of any single group, you had better be sure it does not get into a possible discrimination area. You're much better off to avoid asking or discussing something—even if it's brought up by the candidate, if it involves a person's sex, race, color, religion, national origin, or age.

These are hazy distinctions, I grant you, but the point to keep in mind is that if you're ever called upon to defend yourself against the charge that a certain question or series or questions reduced the chances of hiring a minority or female candidate, you'll have to prove that the answer given *was not* used as a basis for your hiring decision. To repeat, *questions must be job related.* Let's face it, this is the only sensible and fair way to judge people anyway.

Be Careful of Small Talk

One of the biggest problems in the interview process is the occasional innocent question that has absolutely nothing to do with the job opening, or that asks for information the employer will not use in making a hiring decision. Many times such questions are raised in the small talk at the beginning of the interview, for example:

"Are you married?"

"Do you have any kids?"

Are these questions in and of themselves illegal? No, but if you were to use the responses as a reason for your employment decision, then they could be illegal.

Even if you haven't used questions like these to make your decision, merely having asked the question raises the possibility in the applicant's mind that the responses may have been a factor. Litigation could well be the result of such a misconception. You should, therefore, ask job-related questions only. Avoid, at all costs, the seemingly innocent small talk that could lead to a problem later.☑

Winning THE HIRING GAME in the 90's

Do prospective employers still try to "snoop" into the personal lives of applicants by asking prying questions during job interviews? The answer is "yes" according to a poll of 1,007 adults conducted in 1990 by the National Consumers League, a private advocacy group concerned with workplace and marketplace issues. It reported that employers routinely invade the privacy of job applicants by asking questions that have no relationship to job performance. Nearly two out of three respondents, or 65 percent, had been asked their marital status; 46 percent, their off-the-job activities; 23 percent, their religious preference; and 16 percent, whether or not they smoked.

6 LEGAL DOUBLESPEAK

Reference checking puts you between the proverbial rock and a hard place.

Attorneys giving advice on what to tell someone who contacts you about a past employee will advise not giving out any information—except name, rank, and serial number. In other words, provide only dates of employment and job title, and perhaps verify salary level if the caller already knows it. They say it is dangerous to go beyond this data because it could lead to a lawsuit by a dissatisfied past employee.

The very same attorneys will then tell you to get all the information you can about a prospective employee, because employer liability for bad hiring decisions is on the rise. Since the early 1980s, more courts have held companies legally responsible for the actions of their employees, and have gone so far as to point out that a company was actually negligent in the way it went about hiring an individual. Damage awards in such cases can be substantial.

This amounts to legal doublespeak. Don't tell anyone anything when contacted, but expect them to tell you everything when you contact them. In my own reference-checking business, I have been amazed at how often client companies ask me to get all the background data and information about a prospective employee that I can get my hands on; yet, when I contact those same companies to get information for someone else, they tell me that company policy prohibits giving any information to anyone. Everyone from top to bottom seems thoroughly confused by this critical legal issue.

I once asked a prominent attorney why his fellow members of the legal profession would not advise their client companies to start releasing information on past employees in order to balance out the problem. He replied that, in his opinion, lawyers just don't want to admit they've been wrong. Another attorney explained to me that corporate "no-reference" policies probably reflect the influence of ultraconservative legal departments.

I can personally tell you that this business of speaking out of both sides of the mouth doesn't "play well" anymore. Increasingly, I hear attorneys challenged by audience members during presentations they are giving on employment law. Hiring officials ask how they can be told to get all the information they can when considering someone for employment, yet the people they are to get it from are told not to give it to them. One person in the audience compared this situation to a doctor writing a prescription for you, and then telling every druggist in town not to sell you the medicine.

The whole game has become very confusing to everyone, especially those charged with getting or giving out information on employees. They are damned if they do and damned if they don't. An employer is held liable for disclosing too much information, too little information, or for failing to get enough information about the termination of an employee. Many are quite confused and even upset over this conflicting legal advice. There is a school of thought that the legal entanglements we continually create and our inability to deal realistically with them is a serious problem in our country. I wonder if employment law is a prime example of this theory.

Unfortunately, the lawyers consulted on this issue give the traditional advice that has helped to create the present problems in this area: "Get all the information you can, but don't give any." Not only is this poor legal advice, it's terrible management advice. It has led to paranoia in the hiring process and to lies on applications and résumés. Some attorneys who work in this field, however, have been offering a different approach, as we shall see. Everyone is confused on the subject, and even the attorneys are fighting among themselves.

Is it any wonder that the hiring managers with whom I have spoken have made comments such as, "It seems like everything our attorneys tell us just leads to more work for the attorneys." "The lawyers are getting rich from everything connected with employment." And, "Every phase of employment has become a lawyers relief act." In his book, *Million Dollar Habits*, Robert J. Ringer said, "An attorney who graduated at the top of his class at Stanford Law School once told me that his legal education consisted solely of learning how to find problems. Not solve them—*find them.*"[1]

The director of employment at a major U.S. company once said to me, "I'd release more information about our past employees, but the legal department won't let me." I asked him, "Who's running the show anyway, you or the legal department?" As I see it, the legal department's obligation is to clear the way, not block it. They should facilitate the process—not thwart it.

They have in effect rewarded the poor performer and penalized the good one by not revealing pertinent information about someone's past job performance. That's hardly sensible, much less fair. They literally have turned the whole employment game upside down—the bad guys are winning and the good guys are losing.

In New Zealand there is a vine that is especially troublesome. It has small hooks that stick to your clothing, and the more you struggle to free yourself, the more entangled you become. The New Zealanders, who have a sense of humor about such things, call this annoying fact of life on the North Island the "lawyer vine." Has the employment area become our "lawyer vine?"

The Real Problem

I truly believe that we have allowed our employment system to evolve into one that protects poor performers and liars. They know this has happened—and are now taking full advantage of it. I'm sure—unless you fall into that category—this is hardly what you desire, and in fact would like to change as quickly as possible.

In the next chapter, we'll look at how to overcome this mess with ways that are legal, practical, and ethical. ☑

NEW DIRECTIONS IN EMPLOYMENT SCREENING

New views are emerging on the proper exchange of employment information among employers.

talk about hiring issues with many employers, and I also talk with leading attorneys whose practices include labor and employment law. The attorneys emphasize points such as

❏ *Learn as much as you can about a person before you extend a job offer.*

❏ *Don't be afraid to exchange relevant hiring information with your peers.*

❏ *Don't hire if you're unsure about a candidate's past activities and accomplishments.*

Hiring professionals, however, tend to lean the other way. They say things like, "Because we don't give out information except to verify dates of employment and salary level, we don't expect other personnel departments to give us much help either." And, "We feel we can't confront a candidate on the basis of the vague, confused feedback we sometimes get checking references. We don't want to invite a lawsuit."

Courts are showing an increasing willingness to impose liability on employers for the actions of their employees. Declining to make a reasonable background investigation thus exposes a company to the threat of liability to injured third parties.

Hiring managers seem to have lost their will and skill to do reference checking, and this fact is coming back to haunt them. They're confused on how to find out with reasonable certainty how someone acted and performed in his or her previous work setting. Consequently, it is time for companies to get rid of old ideas and start exercising their right to check out job candidates thoroughly. The pendulum is swinging back—from winging it on soft information to digging it out with due diligence.

A New Concern

Attorneys today are very concerned about "negligent hiring," which is the failure to exercise reasonable care and judgment when filling a position. It *is* the employer's responsibility to find out the truth about a potential employee. If the employer chooses to hire an individual without checking his or her background, then the employer must be willing to accept the risk that something might go wrong when that person goes to work. Often, this is a "no-win" situation. For example, if a taxi service hires a driver who assaults a passenger, a lawsuit may result from the driver's conduct. The company may have adequate legal defense but choose to back down to avoid notoriety or simply to spare itself the costs of protracted litigation.

With these legal concerns in mind, companies are sitting down with their attorneys and updating their policies and practices on checking references. The subject is also being discussed in today's business literature as reflected in articles with titles such as, "Negligent Hiring: The Big New Legal Trap,"[1] "Traps for the Unwary Employer;

How to Avoid Exposure to Negligent Hiring Liability,"[2] and "New Lawsuits Expand Employer liability,"[3] which have appeared in major business publications.

As I explain in my seminars on employment screening, negligent hiring is a consideration; frankly though, I have run across very few individuals or companies that got into trouble for something they did (or didn't do) during the hiring process. However, there may be negligence if hired candidates do not work out as expected. Someone hired these mistakes in the first place, meaning that someone or a number of people in the company did not do their jobs well.

This *duty* to check the background of potential employees presents a real challenge to employers as they constantly meet with resistance when checking references. Many attorneys now advise employers to release information with caution. One attorney I spoke with commented, "We are going to have to start being more cooperative [when] giving each other information—particularly if you think you are dealing with someone who might harm someone else." Another attorney told me, "Companies get into trouble if managers speculate on an employee they don't know firsthand, discuss personal issues, or release age or other data subject to discrimination. Firms should 'develop protocol' and stick to it."

Not Giving References

A new potential for liability is that courts may be willing to hold employers liable for "negligent references." In other words, the employer may know that someone has traits that make him or her a menace to others, but fail to disclose the information. A classic case involved a doctor working in a hospital who raped patients while they were under anesthesia. The hospital let the doctor go without saying a word; he ended up in another hospital where he did the same thing.

Each situation has its own set of circumstances. But companies can no longer assume they are safe as long as they say nothing. Failure to state why an employee was dismissed, even if defamatory, may carry as much risk as candidly stating the facts. Most employers have adopted the most conservative possible position, limiting the information they provide to employees' job titles and dates of employment. In doing so, they prevent other employers from gathering information about employees' job histories and work performance—key data in making hiring decisions, data they themselves seek when hiring their own employees.

Of course you can be sued by former employees who believe you gave them bad references. The fear of a defamation suit is neither frivolous nor foolhardy, but the likelihood of such suits has been greatly exaggerated. The flamboyant success of libel suits brought by public figures and tried before juries are more newsworthy than the fact that a substantial majority of these verdicts are overturned on appeal, or that the enormous jury awards are reduced on appeal even if they are not reversed.

Moreover, the picture is quite different in the employment setting. First, it is very difficult for applicants to determine why they were turned down for a job. Second, proving that references were false or made carelessly, recklessly, or maliciously are very difficult criteria for a plaintiff to meet.

If nondisclosure policies continue, they will cause more lawsuits than they prevent. Defamation and invasion of privacy claims will disappear, but negligent hiring and retention suits will replace them.

An old hard-nosed production manager I know has a policy that he openly announces to his employees: If he is ever contacted about them after they leave the company he will be very frank about their job performance. If they were good he will say so; if they were bad he will tell that to anyone who contacts him. He reminds his workers not to let him down or "dog it" just because they think they're leaving the company and it won't matter anyway. I have heard him tell a marginal worker, "I will go out of my way to tell anyone who needs to know that you were a sorry employee when you worked for me." It makes his employees stop and think about whether they want to be described as poor workers, knowing he won't hesitate to relay that opinion to others. And, you know, as far as I can tell, it has been an effective motivational tool for him. Some people might question the legality and fairness of this technique, but what could be more fair to everyone concerned than good old-fashioned truthfulness? We used to call it "telling it like it is."

Employers should examine their policies as to the release of employee information, take advantage of the qualified privilege doctrine, and turn around the trend that is causing negligent hiring lawsuits. Information can be released without being sued if it is done properly.

The Law and Good Business

The law is very much on the side of employers. Employers have a right to discuss their employees with others who have a common interest in them. It's a fundamental legal principle that neither true statements nor statements of opinion can be defamatory, no matter how hurtful they are. Indeed, employers are liable for defamation only if they knowingly or recklessly spread false information.

The bottom line is that it is not illegal to get or to give references. The decision to do one or both should be based on all the factors that influence any normal business decision, such as whether an effort is worth the expected return. Various companies weigh these factors and come to different conclusions. For example, many companies have decided to discontinue company picnics because of the legal and financial danger that such events can create. They looked at the problems that could develop from too much drinking, sports injuries, or whatever else can happen at such unstructured events, and decided it just was no longer worth the effort. Yet, other companies have looked at the same factors and decided they can live with them. The point is that, although there are legal factors to consider, having a company picnic is certainly not illegal.

Should You Give References?

Information about job candidates is exchanged informally all the time. Friends talk to friends; employees of one company talk to employees of another company; managers talk to other managers in their specialty; and certainly executives talk to other executives and even sit on the same boards of directors. Additionally, job seekers often list current members of a company as personal references, which means they want these people to talk freely with potential employers. The point is simply that job-related information is constantly exchanged in the everyday world. As a tough-minded lady employment director said to me, "How the hell do they [most employers] expect us to give former employees a job if they won't talk to us about them?" She and I, along with many others, feel very strongly that it's just not fair to the present or former employees not to talk about them when they are seeking a new job.

Now, as we have been discussing, most attorneys advise against giving substantive reference information about present or former employees to prospective employers. They recommend a most conservative position, limiting the information provided to dates of employment and job title. On the other hand, they advise employers to get all the information they can get when hiring someone.

This type of legal advice bothers many attorneys because it seems to be inconsistent and illogical—which, in fact, it is. Progressive attorneys in the field are now advising employers to give out information while following sound legal and practical guidelines, reasoning that accurate and substantive information about someone's work history is essential to proper decision making by hiring officials. It doesn't make sense to tell an employer to get that information, and then tell the other employers not to give it out when contacted.

Recently, there have been more published articles written by attorneys who now recommend that reference information be given out. Articles on the subject have appeared in national publications, with titles such as, "Employment References—Not a Dangerous Practice,"[4] and "Information, Please: How to Give Useful Job References Without Getting into Hot Water."[5] Clearly, seeds are being planted and more employers are realizing the need and value of giving out reference information. After all, it's done anyway; why not train company members how to do it properly and legally.

One employer I know will, as a matter of policy, actually read over the phone the last performance review of a former employee. I think this is a stroke of genius because it means that a performance evaluation, which we know determines an employee's future in the company, now has an important bearing when the person is making a job change. Knowing this, a person would be foolish to let his performance slip because his poor performance record will be made known to anyone with a legitimate need to know it. Not giving out past performance information encourages mediocrity because it removes a major incentive for trying to maintain a good work record.

By the way, a large number of employers, as a matter of practice, are now giving a copy of the performance review to the employee being rated. Why not ask to see the applicant's last two or three performance reviews? Or, if contacted for information about a past employee, why not suggest that the prospective employer ask to see the candidate's copy of past performance reviews given by your company? This is information that is already developed and doesn't put any reference on the spot about the candidate. Of course, to do this, you need to be confident that you have strong and consistent performance evaluation procedures that you are willing to stand behind.

Another suggestion in regard to giving reference information is to have, as part of the separation process, a form that terminated employees can sign to indicate whether or not they want reference data to be given out after they leave the company. If they allow their employment to be discussed—do it. If they don't, explain that fact to the prospective employer and suggest that the employer review the matter with the candidate to determine why he or she did not authorize such information to be exchanged. Figure 7-1 is a sample release for employment information.

Simplified Guidelines

Tables 7-1 and 7-2 cover the legal interpretations regarding getting and giving references and the basic rules to follow when giving references. They provide a capsulized view of the whole legal issue. This information is general in nature, does not take into account specific state laws or regulations, and is not meant to replace the advice of a qualified attorney in the area of employment law. ☑

Figure 7-1

Sample Release For Employment Information

When the human resource department receives a request for information from a prospective employer about a former employee, we furnish only limited information concerning:

> (a) dates of employment,
> (b) last job title or classification, and
> (c) last applicable wage rate/salary.

We do not discuss orally, or in writing, the individual's work performance, reason for leaving, or any other information we consider to be confidential. This confidential information is divulged only when the past employee has specifically directed us to do so.

Therefore, we would be willing to furnish such additional information if you sign the form below and return it to us. If you do not want us to do this, we will advise the prospective employer that although we can provide such information, you have not authorized us to do so. In either event, this form must be signed and sent to:

Human Resource Manager
The ABC Company
1115 Any Street
Cincinnati, OH

Print Your Name Here: _____

(Sign one space only)

I, hereby authorize the ABC Company to release confidential information concerning my employment record to prospective employers upon their legitimate request for same. I acknowledge that some information divulged may be negative or positive with respect to my performance and agree that I release The ABC Company, its agents, and employees from any and all liability for furnishing such information upon proper request.

_____

(Signature)   **(Date)**

(or)

I, do not authorize The ABC Company to reveal information about my past employment record to anyone, including a prospective employer.

_____

(Signature)   **(Date)**

Source: Certified Reference Checking Company

Table 7-1

Legal Interpretation

*The basic concerns facing employers and the legal basis
for reference checking are outlined below.*

Negligent Hiring

You must take *reasonable care* to get enough information to ensure the new employee will not repeat a deviant past
behavior pattern and cause unnecessary problems on the job.

You must exercise *good judgment* on how much time and
effort to spend obtaining this information.

Reference Checking

Most courts' rulings on reference checking have said that
a *former employer can give information* on a past employee that is *pertinent to making a hiring decision,* as
long as the *information is true or is reasonably believed
to be so.* The law favors the release of background
information. Basically, the *courts in all states* have held
that employers—both former and prospective—have a
"qualified privilege" to discuss an employee's past
performance. As long as the *information is given to
someone with a clear need to receive it,* discussion of an
employee's *past performance—good or bad—is permis-
sible by law.*

This privilege is founded on a policy of promoting
reliable business judgments in hiring—based on all the
knowledge available in the business community. Thus,
when a company releases background information that

enables a potential employer to make a better hiring decision—as long as the statements are true—there is no liability for libel or slander because they were made in furtherance of that *important social policy.*

To comply with equal employment opportunity considerations and rulings, *all questions asked and answers given must be jobrelated*—indicative of the individual's ability to perform the job and of his or her *personality characteristics as they relate to how that person gets along with others in the work setting.*

Table 7-2

Giving References Legally

Defamation of Character

■ *Definition*

Communication to another of information which is false and injurious to the reputation of an employee or former employee.

■ *Examples*

False information about an employee's prior job performance given to a prospective employer.

False information about an employee's character, credit worthiness, or criminal record.

Invasion of Privacy

■ *Definition*

Appropriation of another's name or likeness.

Public disclosure of true, private facts.

■ *Examples*

Using photographs of employees in advertising without obtaining prior consent.

Dissemination of private information such as reason for an employee's discharge, a medical condition, or performance evaluation to those without a need to know.

Legal Guidelines

■ *Procedure:*

1. POLICY—Provide the same type of information for employees at all levels.

2. LEGITIMATE—Communicate only with someone who has a need to know the information, normally a personnel officer or the supervisor to whom the employee will report to on the new job.

3. DOCUMENT—Keep a written record of date interview conducted and the individual(s) spoken with.

4. CONSENT—New employer must have written consent from job candidate to contact references— normally part of signing off the employment application.

■ *Information:*

5. TRUTHFUL—The information must be true to the best of your knowledge with no intent to ruin the person's reputation. It is best if your facts can be supported by proper documentation.

6. JOB RELATED—Limit the information you provide to job-related data only.

7. NOT MALICIOUS—Never provide unnecessary and malicious information just to provide a better understanding of the past employee (or to harm the individual).

8. DON'T VOLUNTEER—Answer only the actual inquiry without opinion or conjecture.

(To win a lawsuit, the candidate would have to prove you violated 5 through 8 above, and there was resulting damage and financial loss.)

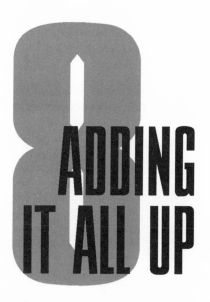

ADDING IT ALL UP

*What we know . . . but don't see
about the legal issues in
checking out job candidates.*

❑ The law *does not* say we *cannot* check the background of those individuals we are thinking of hiring.

❑ There is a very slight danger that releasing information about a past employee could result in a lawsuit, but unless someone's basic rights are violated, there is little chance that the suit would be successful.

❑ *Anything* we do in business can result in a legal problem; in fact, we wouldn't be in business if we were afraid of such complications.

❑ The attorneys who advise us on hiring people are somewhat isolated from the daily problems in the workplace and *do not* have to suffer the consequences of their advice.

❑ The choice to check the references of prospective employees is simply another business decision we have to make.

And in conclusion . . .

❑ These points make it clear that the decision not to check references or not to give reference information is really a matter of choosing *not* to spend the necessary time and effort to do it.

STAYING IN CONTROL
There Is a Much Better Way to Check a Candidate's Honesty—and Faster, Too

HANDLING CANDIDATES

You have to work at making sure people are honest with you.

L et's spend a minute on an important subject. There apparently is something of a trend in this country toward "nice-guy" management. Many managers, for example, write favorable letters of reference for poor employees they want to get rid of, just because it's easier to be nice than to get a little tough and offend someone.

The trouble is that nice guys are sitting ducks for all those dishonest applicants that abound in the land. We know there are those individuals who will say anything—true or false—as long as it helps them reach their goal of getting the job they want. When you evaluate someone for employment, your role is not to make a new friend, but to be sure your company is hiring the right person. You don't have to be a tough guy to do this; in fact, being tough doesn't guarantee that you won't get fooled. What protects you best from being taken advantage of is being completely in control of the hiring process.

What I advocate in handling and screening employees is a style midway between being nice and tough. That is, treat candidates fairly and firmly right down to the words, phrases, and mannerisms you use. You need to take control from the start and stay in control throughout the hiring process. In the coming pages we will show you how to do just that. For some of you it may require being a little more tough minded than you have been.* But if you do what I am going to recommend, it will become quite easy to stay in charge all the way through the hiring process. Success comes from being in complete control.

Listen Aggressively

If you listen and observe other people carefully, they will tell almost everything you want or need to know for you to make enlightened decisions. Even though people are often inconsistent, they do reveal themselves clearly in time. But first you have to know how to *listen*.

Most of us need to listen more and speak less anyway. When interviewing someone or checking references, it is critical to hear what is really being said. Most people literally talk their way out of information simply because they concentrate their attention on what they are saying rather than listening to what others are saying.

Most interviewers are so busy mentally rehearsing the next point or question that they fail to hear what is really being said. This is a very common problem for most people—and a very serious barrier to good communications—because they are neither making a point nor hearing one. Instead, you should talk spontaneously. Probe, question, and follow up until you are fully satisfied with the answers given and feel confident that what you heard is true. In other words, never stop questioning until you have, with reasonable certainty, the information you seek.

---

* For a more complete discussion of tough-minded management and its opposite numbers— nice-guy and tough-guy management, see Gareth Gardiner's *Tough-Minded Management of Problem Employees: Don't Be a Gutless Nice Guy!* (Springfield, IL: Smith Collins Co., 1990).

When listening to someone, we obviously need to pay attention to what's being said. But we also need to listen to *how* it's said. By this I mean voice expression, the real intent, and any hidden clues. I suggest you stop a minute and think of an important conversation you had recently in which there were some underlying or special cues from the speaker that were critical to understanding the message being given. Examples of such cues include a clearing of the throat, a nervous laugh, a long pause, or whatever. You probably picked up on such cues because they were so open and apparent. The secret is to be able to pick them up when they are not so obvious—because they are there if you are alert enough to catch them.

One of the most potent ways to interview someone is to pause or use silence. This technique usually makes the candidate uncomfortable, and he or she may then try to fill the void by providing more information. Most people, when they sense that another person is anxious, try to put him at ease. Anxiety makes people uncomfortable. But if you can learn to allow the other person to be anxious, you may discover something important that you would otherwise have missed. Television interviewers and police officers use this technique with great effectiveness. Try it. You'll be surprised at how most people simply can't stand the sudden quiet, and will rush to give you more details.

Finally, ask the applicant to name other people who can verify the information he or she has given you. This is absolutely critical for two reasons: (1) It tends to keep the respondent honest, and (2) it provides a quick source to contact who will validate what you have been told by the candidate and other references.

Let me sum this up by pointing out that listening to what someone is saying sounds obvious, simple, and easy. But for some reason, probably because the speaker feels the need to impress the listener, this is very difficult for most people to do. If you don't believe me, just observe the next ten conversations in which you are involved, and you will see what I mean.

Ironically, most of the training that I have seen for interviewers emphasizes strong questioning techniques. I truly believe that although the proper questions are important in a good interview, too few interviewers really know how to listen effectively and therefore never really hear what candidates are telling them.

Some interviewers make the mistake of asking too many questions. Don't interrupt but encourage the person to keep talking as you keep listening. Let people unveil their whole stories and allow them to describe for themselves what they think they can do. Listen not only to what the person is saying, but more importantly to what he or she means.

Show the candidate you are listening. Look at his or her face. Lean a little toward the person. These seemingly small body language signals tell someone you are interested in what she has to say. Concentrate on the person's voice. As the person speaks, think about what she is saying. Above all, do not think about what you are going to say in response to the applicant's comments before she finishes speaking. This is probably the greatest mistake you can make. If you are thinking about your next question, you cannot listen to what that person is saying at the moment. Besides, you can easily miss an important point. Even worse, you may miss an important clue about the candidate's honesty.

Spotting Liars

There are two types of lies: prepared lies—when a person readies a false statement ahead of time, and spontaneous lies—when someone responds falsely to an unexpected question. When people lie, their actions often give them away. People who tell prepared lies tend to give very brief answers; answer right after the question is asked; rub their bodies, for example, rubbing their hands together; have tremors in their voices; and sound very rehearsed. People who tell spontaneous lies tend to give brief answers—most liars can't think of what to say quickly enough, make speaking errors such as "we was," or resort to meaningless phrases such as "you know" and "things like that."

Most liars don't want to give a lot of details. The best way "to smoke them out," then, is to ask them to elaborate on what they said. Most liars hate to keep adding to their lies and will usually show it by stumbling around or even completely freezing up. Not every little miscue means someone is lying (people are nervous in interview situations, after all), but if you suspect someone is not being truthful, press harder to see if that is the case. If he or she isn't lying, no one is the worse off, because both of you will have a more credible feeling toward each other. ☑

10 A PROPER INTERVIEW

The interview is the place to identify, discuss, and record the candidate's real references.

I cannot tell you how many times I have gotten reference-checking assignments in my private practice in which the client company has no idea or recommendation as to whom I should contact. The hiring managers have spent hours or even days interviewing and getting to know a prospective employee, yet they cannot name one significant person in the candidate's work life to talk to about the candidate. They have completely missed the opportunity to identify the critical, knowledgeable people who can either verify or refute the information that they have been led to believe is true by the applicant.

We have already established that job seekers are well aware that what they say will probably never be checked out. Most employers leave it up to the candidate to list the people he or she would like contacted as references. The process is slanted toward the applicant, and this needs to be changed. So, let's analyze the interview in its entirety and examine two principles that need to be kept in mind to make the interview a more meaningful exercise for the employer.

How do you do this? It's very simple: Make it very clear during the entire interview that nothing else will be tolerated. In other words, always keep your authority in view.

Our consciences works best when we know we're being watched. What happens when we're driving down the highway and all of a sudden we see a police officer up ahead? Almost by instinct, we lift our foot from the gas pedal, immediately glance at the speedometer, and (if necessary) put our foot on the brake. Or, what happens in a classroom when the teacher leaves the room? Usually, if it's a normal group of students, they start misbehaving.

The most feared words a candidate can hear are, "We *are* going to check your references." This means quite simply, "Be totally honest with us. Distorting your background won't fly here, and only the truth will work in getting the job." Many employers are going so far as to have applicants sign an employment statement (see Figure 10-1 for an example), which they review with each applicant before starting the interview. It will make even the most skillful imposter run for cover. By the way, most attorneys advise that employers have the best protection from lawsuits if the applicant signs a clear release that allows the company to check his or her background and to contact references. If this is set forth in a separate document, rather than by the usual sign-off at the bottom of the employment application, it provides a much stronger legal document. This reduces the danger of someone saying they didn't know what they were signing or were forced to sign in order to be considered for a job.

Warn the applicant up front that all references will be checked. This reminder can go a long way toward making the individual see the need to be honest during the interview. Then, during the interview itself, insist on honest answers by making such statements as the following.

Figure 10-1

Sample Employment Statement and Signature

XYZ Company
123 Any Street
Atlanta, Georgia

Employment Statement and Signature

Date: _____

I have been advised and understand that:

1. The background information supplied by an applicant for a position opening will be checked by XYZ Company or an outside reference-checking service to assure the accuracy of the data furnished and the past performance record of the candidate.

2. I authorize XYZ Company to make such investigations and inquiries of my personal, employment, financial, or medical history and related matters as may be necessary in arriving at its employment decision, I hereby release employers, schools, or persons from all liability in responding to inquiries in connection with my application for employment.

3. I should not resign my current employment until I have received a formal offer of employment, in writing, signed by an XYZ Company Employment Representative.

4. If, for any reason, XYZ Company disqualifies me during pre-employment processing, or at any time prior to starting work, I will be advised of a specific reason only if that reason is health-threatening.

5. The answers given to XYZ Company representatives are true and complete to the best of my knowledge. In the event of employment, any significant misstatements or omissions later discovered in my background may be cause for my dismissal from XYZ Company.

_____   _____
Candidate's Signature   **For the Company**

_____   _____
Print full name   **Title**

_____
Social Security Number

Source: Certified Reference Checking Company

❑ *Answer this question the way you think your reference will.*

❑ *When we call your reference, what do you think he (she) will say?*

❑ *To whom should I talk to verify this point?*

Giving a warning at the beginning, and during the interview, can have a tremendous psychological impact in keeping the applicant honest—and doesn't take any time to do.

Second Principle: Identify and Gather the Names of Meaningful References During the Interviews.

How do you do this? Again it's very simple: You need to identify the key players in the applicant's work life and write them down during the interview. In other words—*choose your own references.*

This is the only realistic way to do it. Otherwise you're letting the candidate furnish the references he chooses—not a very sensible approach. What you end up with are names of the candidate's choosing, such as his minister, brother-in-law, or best friend. This is not to imply that these individuals will not be honest and reliable; however, there are certainly more meaningful people with whom you can speak.

In my private reference-checking practice, I can usually tell if the candidate whose references I am to check has a strong work record just by observing the references given. If the references are previous managers, company officials, or other important people in her work life, then the person is proud of her work history. If the names given are those of close friends, relatives, or others who have never really worked with the candidate, I suspect that she is hiding something. I'm usually right.

The Interview Itself

When I teach interviewing, I emphasize the behavioral-event method of gathering information from the candidate. With this technique, the candidate is asked to relate specific achievements or situations from his or her work career. Sometimes this is also called behavioral-experiences or behavioral-incident questioning.

This technique involves asking simple, probing questions until you literally see the situation or incident in your own mind. Make the applicant relate in vivid detail his or her specific achievements. In other words, get very sound evidence through examples, facts, statistics, and cases, where and when such behavior occurred. Demand evidence about anything that is said. It's all based on the very simple premise that *actions speak louder than words.*

Instead of asking questions such as, "Are you a good leader?" or "Tell me about yourself," and then listening to vague and self-serving generalities, ask for specific achievements and accomplishments. For example, say to the applicant, "Describe to me an actual situation where you were a strong leader," or "Tell me with specific examples why you are better than the other persons we are talking to." Continually probe with follow-up questions until you can literally visualize what you're being told. You can use an open probe—which invites an explanation or ideas—or a closed probe—which requires a simple yes or no answer. The key is to listen actively to understand what action was taken, and then learn what the result was. This in a nutshell is what behavioral-event interviewing is all about.

Now let's add a new dimension: Get the name of a reference or references you can contact to verify the story given by the candidate. *Always identify references during the interview* while the subject or issue being discussed is fresh and clear. Get your reference contact(s) at this time. It's the only sensible approach, but I assure you, very few interviewers do it this way.

There is no reason not to identify at least six references during the interview. Get the names of the applicant's boss and the boss's boss, the names of two peers, and the names of two subordinates or other persons below the level of the candidate at every place the candidate worked. I call it the $2 + 2 + 2 = 6$ formula (Figure 10-2).

Some companies instruct applicants to list on their employment application the names of their previous supervisors with telephone numbers, and then show plainly that these persons will be checked by a member of management. Figure 10-3 illustrates this practice. An employment interviewer I spoke with said that she uses this list of names to identify other candidates that her firm may contact right away or later when they have a suitable opening. Is it legal to do this? Yes. Is it ethical? I don't know, but that's what she does. Just using this system will bring honesty to your hiring program. To see how this whole new checking system can come into play during your interviewing of a job candidate, study the sample background interview form shown in Figure 10-4, found at the end of this chapter.

The Interview in Perspective

An executive in a major international company once described for me his approach to interviewing prospective associates. "I like candidates who turn the interview around and end up interviewing me." I told him this might work well for people in positions of power who like to talk about themselves, but I don't believe it works well for lower-level positions. By the end of the interview, the interviewer may indeed feel that he likes the candidate, but in truth it is only his own image, skillfully mirrored by the interviewee, that he likes. Needless to say, he has learned little about the candidate.

As we have already discussed, another common mistake interviewers make is talking too much. As an interviewer, you must learn the art of engaging another person silently. Remaining silent is difficult for most interviewers, but the general rule is that the interviewee should do about 80 percent of the talking.

Figure 10-2

The 2+2+2=6 Formula

Superiors:

Name/Title **(Boss's Boss)**

Name/Title **(Direct Supervisor)**

Peer: *Candidate:*   *Peer:*

Name/Title   Name   Name/Title
Inside Dept.   **Outside Dept.**

Subordinates:

Name/Title **(Direct Report)**

Name/Title **(Support Worker)**

Source: Certified Reference Checking Company

Figure 10-3

Reference Contacts

MOST RECENT JOBS: (If not applicable, list U.S. Military, or work performed on a voluntary basis, or personal references)

Company _____ Location _____

Phone _____ Job _____

Supervisor _____ Dates Worked: From _____ To _____

Salary _____ Reason For Leaving _____

MGMT. REFERENCE CHECK DONE BY: _____

Company _____ Location _____

Phone _____ Job _____

Supervisor _____ Dates Worked: From _____ To _____

Salary _____ Reason For Leaving _____

MGMT. REFERENCE CHECK DONE BY: _____

Company _____ Location _____

Phone _____ Job _____

Supervisor _____ Dates Worked: From _____ To _____

Salary _____ Reason For Leaving _____

MGMT. REFERENCE CHECK DONE BY: _____

Source: Certified Reference Checking Company

A related mistake is that of engaging in a free-floating conversational interview style. This allows the candidate to discuss her experience largely on her own terms and makes it difficult to compare candidates. For the purpose of comparing responses across individuals, it is therefore best to use a semistructured approach where provisions are made for follow-up questions as needed. A detailed inquiry or a persistent follow-up on an initially general question can bring out critical information about the candidate.

A detailed, semistructured interview should not be a stress-inducing investigation. Some managers conduct stress interviews, expecting that this will allow them to observe how the candidate copes with stress. The problem is that in most cases, the stress produced by this approach is quite different from the stress produced by the job.

Identifying and gathering references during the interview may be stressful for a candidate who has something to hide. Those who are good candidates will have no problem with this. In fact, they will see you as an interviewer who is in control and knows what you're doing. They will see it as a chance for you to learn about the many fine people they have helped and worked with. A poor applicant would rather keep control and steer you to the references of his choosing.

Although this system is seldom used, it really is a sensible way to identify references. Any candidate who has trouble with this is really having trouble with the system's powerful way of getting to the people who know the truth about him or her. Squeezing every ounce of usable information you can out of the interview is just good time management.

Finally, a word about interview impressions. Try as you may to conduct an objective evaluation, an interview is essentially an emotional event. Subjective reactions, whether conscious or unconscious, are inevitable. The interviewer who has a strong like or dislike for an interviewee should ask himself several questions. For example, "Do I like this candidate so much because she is good looking or is there something really positive in her work experience that appeals to me? Or, if I don't like the candidate, is it because she is not my type (different background, culture, race, or just a different person—not like me), or is there something negative in her interview behavior (e.g., guarded, evasive, derisive, or hesitant)? Can I reasonably assume that other people with whom the applicant would have to work will have a similar reaction?" This is a difficult question to answer but, if answered in the negative, may tell you more about yourself than the candidate.

That's why it is so important to check references to see if, in fact, what you think is also what other people have actually observed. However, doing this is never easy and you need all the help you can get in order to do it as quickly and effectively as possible.☑

Figure 10-4

Sample Background Interview

Purpose and Instructions

This background interviewing method relies on a series of simple, probing questions that force an applicant to relate in detail incidents in his/her career: episodes in which, for example, s/he accomplished something on his/her own that made him/her proud, influenced someone, or solved a problem. By analyzing how a person characterizes these events, you can uncover his/her underlying motives and talents.

The interview—which goes right to the critical points—can elicit a person's belief about himself/herself, his/her eagerness to confront challenge and influence people . . . his/her resourcefulness and persistence. Ask open-ended questions, press for examples, and probe the applicant's thoughts and feelings during the event. The best way to find out what you've got on your hands is to suspend judgment and ask sub-questions (if necessary) such as, "Why did you do that? What were you thinking? How did your boss react?, etc."

Like a good detective, your purpose during the interview is not to make a friend, but to get the facts. Keep asking him/her to talk about what s/he actually did . . . his/her actions, accomplishments and achievements. Notice what s/he is wearing, tone of voice, even when s/he smiles. When you finally go over the questions, you may be surprised at the patterns and clues that emerge.

Based on your evaluation and to clear any doubts you may have, call those persons (references) who have been closely involved on the job with the applicant, and can provide further insight into the person.

With this information, the odds are *you will make the right decision!*

Before doing the interview:

Review these 18 questions and circle those you want to use for the opening you have. Example: You may decide to use about half the questions for a lower-level opening and all of them for a key position. Feel free to substitute or add your own questions.

Tell your candidate:

"I will ask you questions that provide an opportunity for you to give me your specific career achievements—to date, and your future expectations—as you see them. I am going to be concentrating on your relevant work experience, knowledge, and competence."

"I will also ask you to provide the names of references you feel will share with me their views regarding your career progress. This is important because I may want to contact specific persons who can verify what we have spoken about during the interview."

Ask the candidate:

1. Exactly why are you interested in this position? How does it fit your career needs at this time?

Sub-Questions (if necessary)
- How did you get into this type of work?
- What do you look for in a job?
- What prompted you to apply for this position?

2. What specific attributes do you possess to be effective in the position?

Sub-Questions (if necessary)
- What unique talents will you bring to us?
- How much do you know about our position opening?
- What sets you apart from the other candidates we will see?

3. What are your long-range career goals and objectives . . . 5 years . . . 10 years?

Sub-Questions (if necessary)
- How important is it to you to reach your goals?
- What are you doing now to achieve those goals?
- What would you like to be earning 5-10 years from now?

4. How has your previous job performance been appraised . . . specific pluses and minuses?

Sub-Questions (if necessary)
- What three areas of your job do you like the most? Least?
- What recent accomplishments are you most proud of?
- How would your last boss describe you?
- Whom can I contact to discuss this with (if needed)?
  Name _____ Phone _____ Company _____

5. Describe a time you felt particularly effective.

Sub-Questions (if necessary)
- What is the most important idea you implemented in your present/last job?
- What was your single most important contribution in your last job?
- What do you think you do best?
- Who would have knowledge of this action (if needed)?
  Name _____ Phone _____ Company _____

6. **Describe a time when you felt ineffective and exactly what you did about it?**

Sub-Questions (if necessary)
- What did you learn from that?
- What was the biggest mistake you ever made in your working career?
- How have you benefited from your previous disappointments?
- Who would have knowledge of this occurrence (if needed)?
 Name _____ Phone _____ Company _____

7. **Describe your last boss.**
 What kind of person is s/he to work for?

Sub-Questions (if necessary)
- Who was the strongest boss you ever had? The weakest?
- Do you prefer to work for a delegator or for one who gives you close supervision?
- What is your boss's title and how often do you get to see him/her?
- Can I contact him/her? If not, who can I talk to (if needed)?
 Name _____ Phone _____ Company _____

8. **How many employees have you supervised in your past assignment(s)?**
 What has been the groups' overall level of performance?

Sub-Questions (if necessary)
- How do you go about establishing rapport with your staff?
- Describe the ideal leader. How do you like being in charge of people?
- Have you had management or leadership training? How did it help you?
- With whom should I speak to review this information (if needed)?
 Name _____ Phone _____ Company _____

9. **Have you had direct hiring authority?**
 How have those you hired worked out?

Sub-Questions (if necessary)
- What do you look for in a job applicant?
- What do other people think about the people you hired?
- What steps do you take to terminate an employee who is not performing adequately?
- Who would have knowledge of this area (if needed)?
 Name _____ Phone _____ Company _____

10. **Were your assignments handled individually or as a group effort? Which role do you enjoy the most?**

Sub-Questions (if necessary)
- What was the most satisfying thing you ever did?
- Have you ever received an award or a citation?
- Give three reasons for your success.

- Who can I discuss this with (if needed)?
  Name _____ Phone _____ Company _____

11. Have you been a reliable employee?
Can you give specific examples to illustrate this?

Sub-Questions (if necessary)
- How many times were you absent in the past year? Year before?
- How often have you changed jobs? Moved or relocated?
- What good personal habits do you have? Bad habits?
- Who can I discuss this with (if needed)?
  Name _____ Phone _____ Company _____

12. How well do you interact with supervisors, peers, and subordinates? Describe which category you enjoy working with the most . . . why?

Sub-Questions (if necessary)
- In what manner do you communicate with your employees? With superiors?
- What do subordinates think are your strengths? Your weaknesses?
- Do you have any close friends at work? What do they do?
- Who can I talk with about this (if needed)?
  Name _____ Phone _____ Company _____

13. What would be the advantage to a new company in hiring you?

Sub-Questions (if necessary)
- Describe the best company you ever worked for.
- What is the biggest single problem your current/past company had?
- If you encountered this situation (describe situation), how would you handle it?
- Who would be able to discuss this with me (if needed)?
  Name _____ Phone _____ Company _____

14. What, in your opinion, is your future growth potential? How far can you go?

Sub-Questions (if necessary)
- How have you changed in the past ten years?
- What would other people say about your potential?
- How important is security to you?
- Who would be the best person to talk with about this (if needed)?
  Name _____ Phone _____ Company _____

15. How can we help you be a top performer?

Sub-Questions (if necessary)
- When do you expect a promotion?
- How long will you stay with our company?

- Who has been the biggest inspiration to you?
- Is there someone who would be helpful to us in this regard (if needed)?
    Name _____ Phone _____ Company _____

16. What is your single strongest characteristic? . . . and your greatest weakness? What are you doing to build on that strength? . . . and what are you doing to reduce the weakness?

Sub-Questions (if necessary)
- In what areas of your present job are you the strongest? Weakest?
- In the past year, what classes, seminars, or conferences have you attended? How many were at your own expense?
- What frustrated you the most in your previous job(s)?
- To whom may we talk to better understand this (if needed)?
    Name _____ Phone _____ Company _____

17. Is there anything in your background that you are not particularly proud of . . . that you'd rather talk about now than have it discovered during our reference checking?

Sub-Questions (if necessary)
- What will your current/previous employer say about you?
- Have any of your employers ever refused to provide a reference for you?
- Would you recommend your current/last employer to others?

18. Is there anything more you would like to contribute to the interview?

Advise the candidate:

At times I may find it valuable to speak with other persons your references may refer me to. Are there any restrictions as to whom I may contact? If so, please tell me their names.

Name _____ Company _____

Name _____ Company _____

How would you rate me as an interviewer?

Interviewer _____ Date _____

YOUR BEST HELPER

The candidate is ready and willing to help if you'll just let him or her.

T he applicant is totally under your control throughout the entire hiring process. You liked the résumé he submitted and selected him to come in for an interview. You asked the questions you wanted, treated the candidate the way you wanted, and decided how long to meet with him. The entire interview was in your hands, and the decision as to whether the applicant was a serious candidate was totally your decision.

Now—You usually let your control end here and take on the full burden of contacting the applicant's references and getting whatever information you think you'll need to be sure of your hiring decision.

But—I say that's not the way to do it.

Instead—It is the candidate's responsibility to personally assist you, as necessary, to verify that the information about his or her work history is correct. Have the candidate contact the references *you* have chosen and ask them to speak freely with you. Then he should ask the references to call you, or arrange an exact time for you to call them. In short, the candidate makes all the arrangements for you to talk with the references. Don't waste your valuable time doing work the candidate can do for you. Let the candidate chase down his references. Also, I suggest having the candidate send his résumé to all the references so that you can ask them if it's correct.

Now I know you're probably thinking, "What about the person who goes to his three or four best friends and sets them up to be the people you want to speak with?" His buddy, Joe, becomes the president of the company; Karen becomes his immediate supervisor; Barry becomes a peer; and Dave becomes his subordinate. To begin with, I can't imagine this being pulled off properly. With any astuteness on the part of the reference checker, using unexpected and thorough questioning techniques (which we will explore in Part IV), this could never happen. Good questioning will immediately stop this farce dead in its tracks. Of course, you can always call the reference back to verify that it was the person to whom you thought you were speaking.

If this still bothers you, then have the candidate call the reference to arrange a convenient (and exact) time for you to contact the reference. Whichever situation you choose, there is no reason that you should spend your time chasing down references when the candidate will gladly do it for you. Why should you care how the reference contact is made as long as you get to talk to the person?

Maybe if we look at it from the standpoint of what's in and what's out, it will become clearer:

What's In . . .

❑ You tell the candidate what references you want to talk with.
❑ The applicant contacts the references you selected and arranges a time to talk.
❑ You get the information you want from the reference and clear up any concern(s) you have.
❑ You are in total control of the reference-checking phase of hiring.

What's Out . . .

❑ The candidate tells you these are the references you can talk to.

❑ You chase down the references the applicant gave you.

❑ The reference tells you what the candidate wants you to hear, and you accept it and don't go any further.

❑ The candidate keeps indirect control of the references you can speak with.

Does using the candidate as your helper work? Let me share just two of the many stories that have been related to me during my nationwide seminars on reference checking.

A line manager at a Midwestern seminar raised his hand and said, "You know, I could just shoot myself after hearing this technique." Startled, I asked him why. He went on to explain that a few months before his company had been getting ready to hire a key manager, and was quite serious about one particular candidate. When that candidate had asked how soon he could start, he was told his references had to be checked first. The candidate then asked who the company wanted to speak with, and was given a list of four people. The candidate volunteered, "If you would like, I can get hold of these people for you, and have them call you." Within three hours all four persons had called and the reference checking was completed. The line manager commented to the seminar group that it never occurred to him to make this practice a permanent part of his employment system, but he was sure going to use it in the future.

During a break at a seminar on the east coast, a lady came up and told me that this new technique really made sense to her, and that she intended to start using it the next day. She went on to explain that getting the applicants to help check their own references had occurred to her but she didn't have the nerve to try it. She then told a story about when she was hired by her company six months previously. She was very excited about joining the company, but it took the company two weeks to check three references. In fact, after the first week, she had called to make sure that she was still in the running for the position. She was assured that she certainly was, but that her reference checks had not been completed. She said she thought to herself that she should offer to contact the references and ask them to call the employer to talk about her. She didn't think that would be appropriate, however, so didn't. She now sees this as a very sensible thing to do.

I can't tell you how much easier this new method has made things for those involved in the employment area. I have had line managers and human resource staff members tell me that this system has made the task of checking references immeasurably easier and quicker. It has literally been the single most important step they have taken in their careers, and it has made their jobs more enjoyable and made them more effective. I have been told by many that they now have time for a nice lunch once in a while, and can even go home on time now.

Getting candidates to help you check their own references is really a useful way to facilitate reference checking. It works because it's a win-win situation. The candidate gets the job right away, and you get your employment duties over with quickly. Good candidates with nothing to hide appreciate it, and, of course, poor candidates who want everything they say to be accepted without question don't like it a bit— it's almost guaranteed to expose them. Once you use it, it becomes a system, and you will see how helpful it can be in your work. In retrospect, it really is rather an obvious idea, but then aren't all really good ideas obvious?

In fact, I have spoken to groups of job seekers involved with outplacement firms and recommended they use the new system to their advantage as job candidates. I tell them that when they learn that they are truly in the running for a position, they should immediately ask if their references will be checked. If so, they should offer to help contact the references in order to ease the burden on the employer and to speed up the process so they can go to work as soon as possible. It's a proactive approach that can help them be viewed as stronger and more viable candidates. Remember this yourself, if you are ever on the other side of the desk as an applicant.

What Are the Advantages?

There are definite advantages to using this new system.

1. By having the applicant ask a reference to speak with you, that person now becomes a personal reference. As we will see in Part IV, this is the only real way you will get consistent, in-depth reference information about your candidate.

2. It solves the legal question of obtaining a release before giving out personal information on someone.

3. The applicant does the contact work for you. You don't waste your valuable time playing telephone tag and then pleading with someone to give you information.

4. It greatly speeds up the hiring process, possibly preventing the loss of a good candidate because you took too long to make your decision.

5. The applicant will see you as someone who is in control of the situation, and will see your company as very thorough and selective in choosing new employees—feeling good about going to work there.

How Honest Are You?

We have just discussed how important it is to insist on and get honest answers from job applicants. But, honesty is a two-way street. Are you being honest with your prospective employees? A recent article in a trade journal made this observation: "Whether unintentional or deliberate, misinforming candidates is a mistake recruiters can't afford to make. Tell candidates what they need to know to make an informed, conscious decision, not what you think they want to hear."[1]

I personally believe and have observed over the years that a lot of the turnover in companies occurs simply because a new employee comes to work and finds out that things are not as she thought or was led to believe they would be. Once on the job, reality sets in and then the person has to decide whether or not this is really the place where she wants to spend her workdays. If the people or conditions are too far from what she expected, she may well decide to leave, and fast.

For example, say you ask an applicant why he left his last job and he says, "I couldn't stand my boss. He was dictatorial, never had a good word for anyone, and cursed at people." Now if this describes almost exactly what his new boss in your company will be like and you don't tell him, what do you think will happen when he comes to work for your company? Or let's say you have a sales opening and you tell the applicant that you have salespeople who earn $100,000 a year and there is no reason she can't be at that level, too. What you don't tell her is that there are two salespeople at this income level and they are the owner's sons who have been given all the old and large accounts. In actuality, the average salesperson earns about a quarter of this after the first year and, in fact, is lucky to make a living for the first six months.

Many times, managers, in their eagerness to fill a vacancy, oversell the job and company. It is easy to find yourself saying things like, "This is a great company to work for," or "You'll really like it here." The anxious applicant wants to believe this, and when someone is hungry, everything looks appetizing. Once hired, though, reality sets in. There is nothing wrong with praising your company, but when you are making the job and company appealing to an applicant, stick to the facts. Describe a typical workday, and be sure to describe the company culture the way it *really* is. New employees soon figure out when they have been misled about the job and may quit as a result.

Deal with firing guidelines. Managers spend a great deal of time telling applicants what qualities and abilities are needed but neglect to outline what is not acceptable. In addition to explaining what qualities you are seeking, tell the applicant what the company won't tolerate. Be honest about the downside, even though you may find it painful to do so.

From the Candidate's Viewpoint

On the other side of the interviewing desk, I also recommend that candidates check out the references of a prospective employer. If you are interviewing for a position in a company, talk to other people who work there or used to work there. Find out why the job is open and speak to the last person who held the position. You have that right as much as the company has the right to check up on you. Don't take the new job if, for example, too many people have recently held the job, the manager is impossible to please, it's full of political battles, there is no clear job description, or too many people tell you it's a bad place to work.

You may want to ask some of the following questions before accepting a position with a new firm:

1. What are the most important responsibilities of this position?

2. What results will be expected of me?

3. What are the limits of my responsibility and authority?

4. What special problems and opportunities are associated with this position?

5. What support is available to help me fulfill the position?

6. Are there any projects in motion which I will inherit? What is their status?

7. What are the goals of this company and my department?

8. Why is this position now open?

9. What advancement can I expect in this company after doing this job well?

Any good book on finding a new job will advise the job seeker how to handle the reference-checking phase of the job search. The most common points usually include:

❑ *Plan who your references will be in advance.*

❑ *Tell them that they may be called.*

❑ *Give them a copy of your résumé so that they are familiar with it.*

❑ *Explain to your references what you are after and how you are selling yourself.*

❑ *And, above all, try to stay in control of whom the reference checker talks with and steer that person only to the references you provide. (In other words, take control of the reference-checking phase from the employer.)*

I personally advise job seekers—assuming they have a good past record—not to let a former employer withhold information about them. I received a call from a desperate lady in Chicago who explained that her past employer, for whom she had worked the previous thirteen years, would not allow anyone to talk about her as a reference. She had been rated as an outstanding employee and had lost her job in a major restructuring and downsizing. I told her to call a senior company official and explain her situation, and ask if he would appreciate this happening to him if he were in her shoes. Obviously, he would see the folly of it all. I advised her to make the former employer talk to the prospective employer, even to the point of taking legal action against her old company.

In fact, I personally go so far as to recommend that, as a candidate, you ask all potential employers if they will provide a reference on your performance with their company in the event you leave or are released. Advise a new employer that you intend to work very hard to be a top performer and expect that this information (or whatever report they have about you) will be relayed, if requested, to a potential employer. If the hiring officer says the company won't say anything good or bad about you, you may want to consider a more progressive company that won't just "file away" those important years of your personal life and career.

Collaboration and Mutual Gain

There is a very simple and obvious reason why the new system will work for everyone concerned. Getting a new employee or job should be a win-win scenario. The company gets a good employee; the employee gets a good job. The hiring process is a way to meet both of these needs. Both parties stand to gain, and both parties are winners.

So what are your options? You can take the position that it's just too difficult to check someone's references and forget doing it completely. You can do it the old way, trying to track down the references yourself and then hope they'll speak to you. Or, you can try the new way, as many have, and enjoy the tremendous results it produces. It's a system designed to help the good candidate, not a way to protect those who don't want their work record checked.

WHAT IT BOILS DOWN TO

What we know . . . but don't see about a new way to check references.

❑ Job seekers believe that whatever they say will *never* be checked out.

❑ When shown that their past record and performance *will be* checked, most job candidates immediately see the need and value of being truthful.

❑ Usually we just can't take the time to track down and convince references to share the information they know about a person with us.

❑ The candidate who really wants the job will do *anything* reasonable we ask to assist the hiring process.

And in conclusion . . .

❑ Based on these observations, there is no reason *not* to have the prospective employee contact the references we want to speak with and make all the arrangements for our reference contact.

Winning
THE HIRING GAME
In The 90s

According to a 1990 survey by the Society for Human Resource Management, 52 percent of employers have increased the amount of time and resources committed to reference checking over the past three years. Seventy one percent check all applicants; 25 percent check some; 59 percent check two references per applicant; while 39 percent check three references. Twenty one percent use outside background investigation agencies, mainly for senior management positions or for personnel who handle money. This is a trend that is likely to continue throughout the 1990s.

TECHNIQUES THAT WORK
Replace Outdated Thinking with Ways That Will Cut Reference-Checking Time in Half—and Double Your Results

TWO ROADS TO TRAVEL

There are a few simple explanations as to why some reference checkers get information and others have difficulty with the task.

here are very effective and workable methods for getting people to speak with you about someone they know. In fact, they are so obvious you might even say they're really not even techniques. Yet, I assure you that most people trying to check references don't realize these techniques exist, let alone use them.

Before we get into exactly what these techniques are, let's look at how information about employees—past and present—is usually exchanged. Information flows back and forth on two levels—formally and informally. There is no way that information can be controlled on the informal level. A friend talking to another friend about someone they both know is one example, as is a manager talking to another manager about a present or past employee, or one employee telling another employee what he or she really thinks about someone with whom they both work. It happens every day at every level, and it's the normal way humans talk to and about each other.

Now, let's look at the formal path for exchanging information between organizations and the people within them; that is, what takes place when one company legally or officially requests information from another company. Getting an official position from a company is usually a complicated and difficult task in which the right officer(s) has to be involved. We all know that getting a company's official position on something takes a lot of time and patience.

On the formal level, under tight controls, a limited amount of information is exchanged. There is virtually an unrestricted flow of information at the informal level, however. The primary difference is that one method functions under rigid company policy whereas the other goes around that policy. While personnel departments can confirm employment dates, job titles, and rates of pay, the best sources of information about an applicant's work habits are peers, subordinates, and former supervisors. It's really this simple and basic.

Let's look at how this works in the employment situation. If you call supervisor John Doe at XYZ Company and ask him about someone who used to work for him, chances are you won't learn much because he has to follow his company's policy on not releasing such information. But if the candidate gives the same supervisor, John Doe, as his personal reference, and you call and advise Mr. Doe that he has been given as a personal reference for the applicant, the chances are that he will see the situation in a whole different light and cooperate fully with you.

Under the formal method you get little or no information because of legal or other fears, such as possibly giving the wrong information or not representing the company properly. With the informal method, you will probably get natural and insightful comments and observations that are quite valuable. Obviously, of the two roads to travel, the informal one is most likely to get you where you want to go.

The real reason the formal road is painfully slow to travel is because it's a case of one company trying to talk to another company, which is virtually impossible. You don't call companies—you call people. The informal road is easier to traverse because it's one person talking to another person—the only way things get done. Figure 13-1 summarizes graphically what we have been talking about.

Why Give References?

There are very good business and common-sense reasons for giving reference information on former employees. Yet, I am always amazed how often these reasons are ignored or overlooked, even by human resource professionals and business managers who should know better. These reasons include:

1. *Giving references continues company-paid outplacement assistance.* Companies paying for expensive outplacement assistance for a former employee who was fired or released due to downsizing often won't cooperate with a new employer who may be interested in hiring this person. I actually called a company that was paying in the range of $20,000 for outplacement assistance for one of its separated executives, and was told it couldn't provide any information about the individual. Paying for such professional help and then hindering the process of helping ex-employees get new jobs, especially when their job-seeking efforts start coming together, hardly makes sense!

2. *It lowers unemployment costs.* Unemployment rates in most states are based on how long former employees are unemployed and have been drawing unemployment assistance. The quicker these individuals get back to work, the lower your unemployment tax rate will be, so why not cooperate fully with a new employer who may put the unemployed person back into the work force?

3. *It ends an unpleasant situation.* When someone is terminated, for whatever reason, it's tough emotionally on everyone involved. Unemployed people are often not happy and tend to look backwards, blaming their last employer for not fully appreciating or

Figure 13-1

Two Roads to Travel

Person to Person

Method	Pattern	Result
Friend to friend	Unrestricted flow of information	Insightful comments and observations
Manager to manager	Not controlled	Very valuable
Employee to employee	Avoids company policy	
Employee to personal reference		
Employee to other references		

INFORMAL

GOOD BUSINESS

COMMON SENSE

Open Road—Some Detours

Company to Company

Method	Pattern	Result
Personnel dept. to personnel dept.	Very limited amount of information	Little or no information
Company to company	Rigidly controlled	Limited value
	Per company policy	

FORMAL

LEGAL

FEARS

Road Blocks

using their talents. The previous employer is trying to get on with business and let bygones be bygones. The easiest way for this to happen is to help ex-employees find new jobs.

3. *It provides a reward for good performance . . . and a penalty for poor performance.* Let's suppose someone worked for you the past ten years and was a very loyal, productive, and reliable employee who always received top performance ratings; however, she had to be released when the firm reorganized. Another employee—who was employed approximately the same amount of time but had a bad attitude, low productivity, and high absentee-ism—also had to be let go, which was something you had wanted to do for a long time anyway. If someone were to call you about these two people, and under your company policy you aren't allowed to say anything, it sounds like both have the same level of performance. The top employee doesn't receive any credit for being good and the marginal employee is not penalized for her poor work record. What could be more unfair?

Look at the Real World

In fact, the policy of not giving out reference information about a past employee, established by the human resource departments of nearly every company, is ignored by most people. I can tell you as an experienced reference checker that people really want to provide information about someone; you just need to give them a good reason and make it easy to do so. When I contact references, I get about 90 percent cooperation. No more than one out of ten just won't respond or help at all. Although the rules of the game set by most companies forbid talking about someone's personality and performance, most people will not play this game.

If one of your company's executives meets an executive from another company at the local country club (where they both have company-paid memberships) and is asked her opinion about someone who used to work at your company, do you think she will reply that she can't say anything due to your nondisclosure policy, and that the other executive will have to call the personnel department? Or, if one of your foremen meets a foreman from another company at the bowling alley (where they are both on company-sponsored teams) and asks about a former employee of yours he is thinking of hiring, do you think your foreman will cite company policy and tell him to call personnel? If you do, you are suffering from a bad case of naiveté and have lost touch with the real world.

The overwhelming majority of people will be honest with you if you ask them the right questions. It's easy to detect when someone is lying for someone else, as we will see later. I personally received a call about a person I had worked closely with at a large *Fortune* Top 50 employer. I was asked to talk about him and responded by giving his strong points—professionally and personally. Never once was I asked if there were any shortcomings or recommended improvement areas. Yet, there were some and, if asked, I would have explained them. Indeed, I would have said I would not hire the person! But I was not asked.

There are three basic premises that apply to the world of reference checking.

1. The chances are overwhelming that a person will not—
   • perform any better,
   • work any harder, or
   • act any different
   —for you than he or she has done for others in the past.

2. The most powerful tool in business is information because good managers given good information can make good decisions. When making an all-important hiring decision, you need the best information you can get.

3. In the long run, instincts are no match for information. There is a no more certain recipe for disaster than a decision based on emotion.

Checking References: The Positive Aspects

I truly believe that the real basis for being successful in checking references is a positive feeling about the task on the part of the person doing the checking. Unfortunately, most of those assigned to check references don't like doing it. At the beginning of my seminars on the subject, I ask how many participants really enjoy checking references. Naturally I raise my own hand, but out of a group of 50 or more, I usually find no more than 2 to 3 people who also enjoy doing it.

As I see it, the problem is that it's hard to be good at something you don't enjoy doing. Unless I can show you that checking references is a very positive action, and that you can actually have fun doing it, you won't be very successful. A negative feeling about something you are trying to do is immediately transmitted to others, and this feeling is probably why most people who attempt to check references are not successful.

What are the positive aspects of checking references?

1. Reference checking provides clear testimonials to support your decision to hire a particular person. Let's face it, if the references check out, you'll feel much better about the judgment you made.

2. It gives justice where justice is due. In other words, you'll hear good things about good people, and poor things about marginal performers. As we said before, good people are literally penalized when we don't talk about them.

3. It may provide additional evidence of accomplishments or factors not covered in the interview. Every time I check references on someone, I hear favorable points about the person that weren't brought out during the interview, such as he's a good family man, she's very religious, he doesn't smoke or drink, she's not a substance abuser, he runs three miles every day, and many other factors that aren't part of the interview—yet reflect well on the applicant.

4. It gives you management-development advice that enables you to best fit the person into your organization. All of us have flat spots, and if you're doing a good job checking references, you will discover them. It has often been said that our greatest strengths are also our greatest weaknesses. For example, if someone is very aggressive, you need to look at the other side and see how sensitive he is to others. If someone works very hard and puts in long hours, she may not be a good delegator.

A reference check I conducted on a candidate for the position of plant manager (who at the time was a plant manager with another company) indicated that he was totally dedicated to his work, usually working ten or more hours a day and four to five hours on Saturdays and Sundays. All four of the references I contacted felt that he was a great manager who was very effective; however, they also said he had better slow down before he had a heart attack. They all commented that he really needed to learn to delegate more. When he started the new job, he was told what his best friends had said about him and it had quite an impact. In fact, he and his new supervisor developed a plan of action to change these personality and management flaws.

The more you know about someone in advance, the better you will be able to guide and help him or her succeed in your company. What you learn about someone up front is what you will find out in three months, six months, or a year or so after he or she has been working for you. Isn't it better to discover it sooner rather than later and proactively address the situation, rather than react later on?

5. Effective reference checking establishes you as someone who can protect your company from a poor hiring decision. A company invests a considerable amount of time, money, and energy in hiring and training a new employee and if, for whatever reason, the new person doesn't work out—the cost skyrockets. An employee who fails and leaves after a few months can cost a company anywhere from $5,000—for an hourly worker—to $75,000—for a manager—in lost productivity and money spent on training, to say nothing of lowered morale and profits. If you can sit in front of a hiring manager and present solid facts and opinions to support the hiring decision, you will be viewed as a valuable member of the company.

I am a firm believer that you won't be effective at checking references unless you see the positive side of it. All the techniques we are going to look at in the coming pages won't make you effective in this function unless you believe you are doing something very necessary and positive for your company, as well as for the candidate. No one gains from a poor hiring match, and, in particular, the reputations of those who let it happen will suffer.

Types of Checking

There are two types of background checks: the record check and the reference check.

The record check determines honesty. The record check is one that can be performed by secretaries or clerical personnel to determine whether the data the applicant has given is accurate. It is nothing more than confirming that the previous dates of employment, job titles, academic degrees, professional license(s), and such are accurate. In fact, the people who relay the information may never have met the person in question. Unfortunately, this is as far as many companies go in their checking—usually calling it reference checking, which is not accurate.

The reference check determines competency on the job. This phase of checking gets into candidates' ability to conduct themselves appropriately as well as their job performance, and is usually carried out by the employment staff or hiring manager. This involves an in-depth conversation with someone who knows and/or has worked with a particular candidate. It gets into one, two, or three areas of personal conduct, depending on how far you want to go, with an increasing level of difficulty the further you delve into the person's background, as shown below.

❏ *Sociability:* *How well the candidate gets along with and relates to other people. This information is fairly easy to discuss and discover and can usually be obtained from anyone you speak with—both personal and professional references.*

❏ *Work habits and ability:* *How well the applicant knows his work and performs on the job. You want to assess the person's technical or functional ability, and the attitude he has on the job. Obviously, this information has to come from people who have worked with the person, such as fellow employees, peers, subordinates, supervisors, or company officials.*

❏ *Personal character:* *What are the candidate's basic beliefs, morals, and ethics? This level of information may be desired in a key or very sensitive position and will have to come from talking to the people we mentioned above as well as close friends, secretaries, or neighbors. In fact, it may move beyond normal reference checking into a private investigation or a background investigation for a security clearance.*

Certified Reference Checking Co. conducted a survey of 72 major companies in the Midwest, asking them the extent of checking they do as we just defined it. The subject was discussed in-depth during seminars on hiring new employees, and participants were asked to indicate by a show of hands how deeply they actually checked the background of their job applicants. Companies responded as shown in Figure 13-2.

Figure 13-2

Survey: Depth of Checking

58%
Record &
Reference
Checks

32% Record Checks Only

10% No Checks

Source: Certified Reference Checking Company

14
REFERENCE-CHECKING TECHNIQUES

A positive attitude about reference checking, coupled with good techniques, will produce wondrous results.

efore we get into specific techniques that will make you a successful reference checker, let's take a look at the basic reference contact itself. I'm sure by now you're convinced that you should contact the references you choose, not just the ones the candidate gave you to contact. Additionally, you can develop new references from the references that you do contact. There is no law anywhere that says you must contact only the references the applicant gave or wants you to speak with.

If you have spoken with a number of references, and then a new reference points out something of concern, go back to those you previously spoke with and review the matter with them. For example, you called the first reference and there were no special problems. You talked with reference number two, and she also said everything was all right. Then you call reference number three, who indicates the applicant was absent from work a lot, possibly due to a chemical-abuse problem for which he eventually underwent treatment. Now most people would immediately think that they should call some more references to get a handle on this—which you may want to do. However, you have already established a telephone relationship with the earlier references, so why not call them back—remind them of your initial contact—and explain that something has come up since your earlier conversation on which you need to get their views. Then explain the issue to them. You'll be surprised how quickly they'll tune in and try to help you, because in a way you're putting them on the spot and testing their basic credibility. Contacting references a second time to clarify questionable information that later comes to light is a sensible, yet underused reference-contact method.

Getting sufficient time to speak with a reference contact is a frequent problem. A typical reference call may last 10 to 45 minutes, a significant slice out of someone's workday. Therefore, it may be necessary or advisable to call references at home during the evening or over a weekend to get the information you need. There is usually a noticeable difference in the way people respond when they're at home. They are more natural and relaxed and can give you the uninterrupted time you need to discuss the candid in question. Most people at work are under heavy time pressure and may be afraid of being overheard because they feel as if they're representing their company, rather than speaking personally about the candidate. You don't get good responses when someone's mind is somewhere else. Therefore, you need to eliminate all the distractions you possibly can.

Occasionally, I have spoken with references at work and then had to finish the conversation when they got home; I've found that it is almost like talking to two different people. At home people are much more relaxed and responsive to my questions and are often more willing to elaborate. It's always better to have too much time, rather than not enough. In my private reference-checking practice, I make about 40 percent of my calls after work hours and on weekends to people at home. I never hesitate to call anyone at home—in the evenings, on weekends, or holidays—and have never run into any resentment to my call.

Now I realize those who work a normal workday can't spend all their evenings and free time contacting references. However, in special cases and for critical openings, it may be important to make that sacrifice for your employer. An employment manager at one of my seminars said that because it is so much more effective, she encourages her staff members to make after-hours reference calls, and gives them compensating time off for doing so. She added that she can tell if her staff has put in the time by the content of the report they provide to her.

Introducing Yourself with Impact

When making your initial contact with a reference, you should take charge quickly because the first inclination of the person will normally be not to participate in the reference contact if there is a way out of it. The reason for this reaction is the negative legal aura that has surrounded reference checking and the resulting fear that you can get into trouble for what you say. Additionally, most people would just as soon not get involved in a discussion about someone they know for fear that what they say could get back to the person. So, like it or not, there is almost an inborn fear about serving as a reference for someone looking for a job.

The way to start your reference contact is to tell the person that the candidate (by name) has asked (if that's the case) or authorized you to contact him or her to verify information already given. For help in visualizing this introduction sequence, please note the accompanying work script in Figure 14-1. Explain to the reference that a job offer will not be made until you can verify the candidate's background. In most cases, this is all you need to say to get the reference's cooperation. If this doesn't work, there are other useful statements you can make.

Another way to get cooperation is to ask the reference if he would like a personal call from the candidate authorizing him to speak to you. About 80 percent of the time, the reference will tell you that won't be necessary because he doesn't want to bother or alert the candidate about his reluctance to speak with you. I find that most people agree to start talking after I make this statement.

Figure 14-1

Introduce Yourself

If Reference Answers:

● *Mr./Ms. _____ , my name is _____ with XYZ Company.*

● *We are in the process of hiring _____ .*

  • *Before we will extend an offer, we need to verify his/her background.*
  • *S/he has asked that we contact you as his/her personal reference.*
     OR
  • *S/he has given us approval to speak with you as his/her (personal) reference.*

● *I would like to spend a few minutes with you. Is this a convenient time to talk? (If not) when would be the best time/day? At work/home?*

  • *I will call you then.*
     OR
  • *I will look forward to your call.*

  (Thank you.)

● *Everything we talk about is confidential and will be treated that way.*

If reference is not in:

● *This is a personal call. When will s/he be in?*
● *Please have him/her call me at _____ .*
        OR
● *A friend of his/her has given him/her as a personal reference and I need to speak with him/her as soon as possible. When should I call him/her?*

If reference will not cooperate:

● *Ask the reference if s/he would like a personal call from the candidate authorizing him/her to speak with you.*

● *Tell the reference that his/her unwillingness to speak with you must mean that it would be a bad reference.*

● *Advise the reference that by not speaking to you s/he could be legally liable for the candidate not getting the job.*

Fallback (Comment):

"I can't understand why we're having a problem getting you to talk with us, because we're just trying to help _____ get a new job. Who can I talk with to clear this matter up?

Source: Certified Reference Checking Company

If these two openings don't work, you might tell the person that her unwillingness to speak with you must mean that it will be a bad reference. Then let the reference defend her position. You can further ask if her refusal to talk about the candidate applies only to this particular candidate or to all former employees.

As a last resort, you might pressure the person to cooperate by advising the reference that by not speaking with you, he could be held legally liable for the candidate *not* getting the job. Sound farfetched? It isn't! I have personally advised a few people, who had a previous employer that would not speak about their employment at the company, to consider legal action against that employer for interfering with their actions to get a new job—and I think you may see more of this as a reaction to employer nondisclosure policies. Another new potential for liability is that courts may be willing to hold employers liable for "negligent references." In other words, the employer may know that someone has traits that make him or her a menace to others, but fail to disclose the information. Employers should be aware of a growing body of law concerning "failure to warn." In some states, if a former employer, when contacted by a potential employer, fails to warn of some facts about the employee that affect public safety (such as a truck driver fired for repeatedly driving while intoxicated), the former employer may be held liable if the employee causes injury due to the fact or condition not disclosed. Failure to state why one has been dismissed, even if defamatory, may carry as much risk (or more) as candidly setting forth the facts.

There is always a final fallback comment, which involves exclaiming that you just can't understand why you're having a problem getting the reference to speak with you, because all you're trying to do is help someone she knows get a new job. Then ask who you can talk with to clear this up.

Take Charge Quickly

Once you reach the reference contact, take immediate control to assure that the time spent by both you and the reference is not wasted and produces meaningful information. One very important point must always be kept in mind, however. When you call people on the phone, you are literally interrupting them somewhere in their workday. All of us have a scale of emotions we go through in a given day that ranges from being happy to being stressed out, and everywhere in between. You will be making contact with that person somewhere along the emotional scale, which you won't know beforehand, and you have to be sensitive to where he or she is now. For example, if the person you contact just came out of a difficult meeting with her boss, she may be nervous and not fully focused on your call. On the other hand, if she just came out of the boss's office after receiving a big raise, you will probably have a much more cooperative reference. See the point? You will be catching everyone somewhere along their range of emotions and you need to adjust quickly. This is common knowledge to sales-people and others who deal with the public all the time; however, it may not be fully recognized by those strictly administrative types of people who are paid to process information as quickly as possible. They tend to see all their tools, and even other people, as only a means to get their job done. Always remember when you ask for a reference that the person you're talking to is doing you a favor. Politeness counts, and you must always keep that in mind. Also, be sure that you are in the proper emotional state; when you're upset, you don't see things clearly.

The following rules may help you reach your goal of getting a reference to cooperate with you.

1. *Take a totally assumptive approach.* Remember that you are sincerely trying to see your company and the candidate come together. Be absolutely surprised when someone doesn't cooperate. Set the stage for forthright talk. Say, for example, "I want to be fair with Ms. Brown. If we hire her and she can't do the job properly, or doesn't fit into our organization, we'll have to replace

her. This could damage what appears to be a very nice record. That's why I'd appreciate it if you would help Ms. Brown and me by being candid in your response to a few questions."

2. *Be relaxed, calm, and courteous.* Don't be rushed. You are asking someone to give you his or her valuable time.

3. *Explain the purpose of the call.* Tell the reference that an offer cannot be made unless references are checked, and that the candidate has asked or authorized you to talk with him.

4. *Ask permission to continue the call.* Inform the reference, "I will need about ten minutes of your time. Is this a good time to talk?"

5. *Expand your information.* Start with verification questions—then move to performance, developmental, and networking questions—which we will look at in more detail later. Continually probe to gain insight.

6. *Don't assume anything.* Listen reflectively and ask for clarification and intent. Learn exactly what the reference is telling you. It's much better to have too much information than not enough.

The Voice's Body Language

It's better to telephone than to write when checking references because you can often detect enthusiasm, or lack of it, if you pay attention to "voice language." Moreover, you can ask for amplification of limited answers to your key questions. The very best way, when practical, is to go in person. An eyeball-to-eyeball visit produces the most revealing responses, including the opportunity to absorb important nuances—such things as raised eyebrows, deep sighs, or dubious expressions.

Probably about 35 percent of what we learn comes from the voice's body language. What is said obviously is important, but even more important is how it's said, as well as what is not said. We have all been around long enough to know that body language really communicates a person's innermost thoughts to us. Well, the voice does the same thing as you will note in the examples below.

The Sweeping Statement: "She was the greatest employee we ever had."
Lesson: Be careful of exaggerations or absolutes. Ask the reference to support such statements with more specific information on the subject being discussed.

Hedging Through Hesitation: "Let me see how I can put this."
Lesson: Advise the reference to be objective and truthful in order for you to determine that your decision is right for both the candidate and the company.

It Wasn't All His Fault: "I guess it was a big misunderstanding."
Lesson: Let the reference know that you have to focus on the person's specific actions regarding what happened.

Obvious Avoidance: "I'd prefer not to comment on that."
Lesson: Ask why the reference won't comment. Explain that you have to understand everything about the candidate in order to make your decision.

Telltale Inflections: "Uh . . . ah, yeah . . . he was honest."
Lesson: Insist that the reference comment further, explaining that you have to be accurate and precise in the information you assemble about someone.

When checking references, *never* assume *anything*. If you're not sure of something, continue to probe until you feel you are being told everything you need to know about the subject in question and understand it thoroughly. If you don't understand something, continue to ask questions until you can actually sense and see the answer you are being given. If the information is not forthcoming, ask for more information or clarification, with follow-up questions such as, "Would you please give me some examples of his accomplishments in that area." "Please explain that further." "I'm having a hard time understanding what you're telling me and need to stay on this subject." Ask follow-up questions in your own language and style. But the point is, don't stop asking questions until you are sure that you understand totally what you're being told. Above all, don't allow yourself to be "snowed" or misled about a candidate's real qualities and qualifications.

In my private reference-checking practice, I have run across some strange and fascinating answers. In one instance I asked if the reference was honest. There was a long pause, and the reference answered, "As honest as the next person." I then asked, "How honest is the next person?" Another long pause, then came the reply, "As honest as most of us." What I finally sensed was that I had a dishonest person trying to cover his own and the candidate's unethical behavior. My favorite answer is, "He was too light (or too heavy) for that." Finally, after hearing this answer so often, I started asking if the reference thought that the candidate didn't weigh enough (or weighed too much) and needed to change his diet. After laughing, the reference will explain in better terms what he or she really means, that the person is either overqualified or underqualified for the position. I was once told that a candidate had left the company because of "organization dynamics." When I asked the reference to explain what he meant by that phrase, I found out it meant that the applicant couldn't get along with other people in the company.

Letters of Recommendation

Letters of recommendation are becoming increasingly unreliable as a means of evaluating job candidates. For one thing, they can be faked. In all but the rarest of cases, a letter is apt to be favorable, even when the writer knows the candidate is mediocre or unqualified. This is so because the writer knows the candidate will read the letter, and perhaps even sue if the contents are not to his or her liking or insufficiently substantiated.

When checking references, do not rely on written documents presented by candidates. This method is virtually worthless. The references were probably written at the time of termination and the employer, feeling bad about it, laid on the praise. How many negative letters of reference have you seen?

Let's say that one of your employees has decided to pull up roots and relocate to another part of the country. Because he doesn't know what companies he'll be applying to, he asks you for a letter addressed "to whom it may concern" to attach to his résumé. You can now do one of three things: (*a*) Write a glowing reference, sign it, and send him on his way; (*b*) ask him to write the letter—review it, change a few minor points, and return it; or, more advisably, (*c*) tell him a reference letter is too impersonal, and you'd much rather talk to prospective employers so you can tailor your comments to their job requirements. There really is no better way to get or give reliable information about a candidate than to talk with the people who have had close contact with him or her.

Now, on the humorous side, if you want to convey unfavorable information in a way that the candidate cannot perceive it or prove it as such, you can write: (to describe a person who is woefully inept), "I most enthusiastically recommend this individual with no qualifications whatsoever." To describe someone who is not particularly industrious: "In my opinion you will be very fortunate to get this person to work for you." Or, for a candidate who is not worth further consideration: "I would urge you to waste no time in making this person an offer of employment." But such ploys won't be necessary if you personally speak with the prospective employer.

Sphere of Influence

References will lead you to other references. In general, however, all references do not have the same degree of influence on your hiring decision. Figure 14-2 illustrates the sphere of influence of references.

Normally you will start out with the references the candidate gave you, or preferably the references you have identified during the interview as people you want to speak with about the candidate. This is the inner circle of people close to the candidate, with whom the candidate may have spoken and perhaps even suggested what they should say. However, these references can lead you to the neutrals, that is, people who will freely express their views—good or bad—about the candidate. And they, in turn, may even point out detractors, people who don't like or get along with the candidate.

The way to get this to happen is simply to ask at the end of each reference contact whether the reference can think of or recommend anyone else with whom you should also speak. Believe me, that's all there is to it, and it works. It's nothing more than the simple networking of your reference contacts. Then, of course, based on the individual situation, you can decide if you want to make the additional contacts.

Networking references is the most effective way of going after the special information you want, or to keep from being "blind sided" by a pre-arranged reference. And, as we have seen, there is no law in any state that says you have to talk only to the references the candidate gave you. You can continue the process as long as you feel it's necessary.

Nobody's Talking

What happens when, no matter how hard you try, you just can't get people to talk about a job candidate? Do you give up and take the attitude that many line managers and employment specialists take— that checking references is just too difficult and usually doesn't work, so it should be abandoned as part of their employment process?

Believe me, with a little extra initiative you can make reference checking work for you, allowing you to get the information needed to make a proper hiring decision, using these simple actions.

Expand (and raise) your contact level. If you *don't* want in-depth information about someone, call the personnel department. Its job is to enforce the company's no-information policy. A personnel department usually won't give you anything beyond the former employee's

Figure 14-2

Sphere of Influence

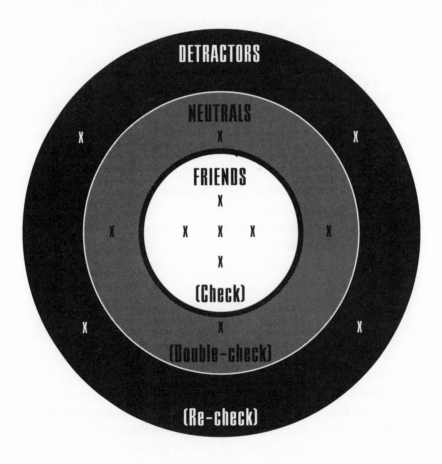

Source: Certified Reference Checking Company

dates of employment, previous job title, and possibly confirm the last salary, sometimes only doing this in writing. In many cases, personnel department staff have never worked with the candidate and may never have even met him. You know going in this may happen, so don't be surprised when it does.

Obviously, what you have to do is expand your contacts to key members of the company who have worked with the candidate. These can be subordinates, peers, or supervisors. I can tell you from years of experience that this is all you have to do. I can also tell you that the higher people are in the organization, the easier they are to talk to. In fact, upper managers act like they don't even know there is a company policy against giving out information about former employees or people who currently work for the company. In most instances, they will freely discuss and comment on the strengths and weaknesses of the person in question in a very courteous and helpful way.

The easiest reference checks I encounter involve talking to high-level executives. They instinctively know that the exchange of information is a vital aspect of business life, plus they sense that there are good business and common sense reasons for giving references, as we mentioned earlier. Obviously, you need to stick with people who personally know or who have worked closely with the candidate, but that's the only limitation you have. Don't call the chairman of a company about everyone who has ever worked there. But, do call him if the candidate reported directly or even indirectly to him.

In fact, when I have problems with personnel staff specialists or line managers who don't want to cooperate, I frequently call the top human resource officer and explain my dilemma. Almost without exception, he or she will direct me by name to someone within the company. When I call that person, I advise who suggested I contact her, and she is then very willing to talk to me.

Check your own employees. You would be surprised how often you have employees who know or who have worked with the candidate. During the interview, when the candidate wants to tell you anything you want to hear, ask if he has any relatives or knows anyone who works at your company. Write down their names, and, especially if you're with a large company, you may have all the reference contacts you need without having to make an outside call.

Confront the candidates. What if information just isn't flowing back to you, but you're still interested in a certain applicant? Go back and advise the candidate that both of you have a problem—that you can't offer her a job until you have satisfactorily checked her references, and that unless something can be worked out, she won't get the position. Then you mutually identify references and determine how you will get them to speak with you. As we have been discussing, have her do the work for you in tracking down and getting these people to talk with you. A good candidate will welcome that role.

Don't Call My Employer

In my national seminars, the question is always asked, "What do I do when the candidate is currently employed and I can't call his current employer because it will jeopardize his present job?" I always point out that any time people are in the job market, they are taking a calculated risk that their present employer may find out they are looking. However, I agree that in such a case you certainly don't want to do anything that would knowingly jeopardize their current job.

The solution is rather easy. Identify, with the candidate, persons with whom he or she worked at the company who are no longer there, such as those who recently left for new employment or recently retired. Every company has some turnover. There are also customers, clients, and even vendors who can be contacted. Additionally, you would be surprised how often fellow employees and even the person's supervisor know he is looking for a new job. If you ask the candidate, he will usually be able to supply the names of current fellow employees who can be trusted enough "not to spill the beans."

The use of former employees or retirees as references is an excellent practice today. Companies have unloaded thousands of people who can readily be contacted. Because they are no longer connected with the company, they are usually more than willing to talk freely and openly about someone with whom they used to work. I find I am using these people more often as my reference contacts; in fact, in some cases they have been my primary source of references regarding contacts.

You don't have to and shouldn't ignore your reference-checking responsibility just because someone is currently employed. With a little initiative on your part, the situation can be properly handled. There is never a reason not to check someone's references.

Getting Personal

Remember, every reference is a personal reference because everyone you talk with knows the candidate personally! As we saw earlier, to be effective you must talk with references on a person-to-person basis. Virtually no one will give you the official company position on someone they know; however, they can certainly give you their personal view.

The best way to get this person-to-person connection is to identify, and stress when introducing yourself, that the candidate has named this person as a personal reference, if that is the case. Alternatively, advise the person that she has been given as a personal reference for the candidate, or the candidate has authorized you to talk with his personal references. Some people feel this is being tricky, but I don't agree; everyone you speak with knows the candidate personally, and they are speaking only for themselves. If this liberal interpretation bothers you, don't use it; however, you will lose a very effective way to establish a relationship with the reference contact.

If you must leave a message requesting a call back by the reference, you will get a much better response if you explain the importance of returning your call. Now that many companies use voice mail to field incoming calls, when you dial someone you may get a recorded voice suggesting you leave a message, instead of a live person. The good news is that you can access this equipment 24 hours a day, 7 days a week. The bad news is that you are faced with the reality that you're not going to talk with the reference unless he takes the initiative. To get his help and cooperation, leave a message explaining that he has been given as a personal reference, and you need to speak with him as soon as possible. Convince the reference that his valuable time and information is vital to Mr. or Ms. Candidate getting a new job. Sometimes you may be able to find a secretary to relay the message to the reference.

Value of Personal References

Now let's talk about the real personal references, those individuals actually listed on the employment application by the applicant. Most employment professionals advise against using these references because they are most likely friends of the applicant who have been programmed to say nothing but favorable things. I personally don't agree with this line of thinking because these people can be very valuable sources of information, for the following reasons.

1. Most people don't want to get involved in lying—even to help a friend. I am convinced that, with a few exceptions, people aren't comfortable lying and don't want to lie for someone. If you ask the right questions, they will be honest with you. In fact, I have actually had personal references given by the candidate tell me that something the candidate said was false or badly misleading. Even personal friends are not eager to lie for someone, and go out of their way surprisingly often to set the record straight.

2. Personal references are usually not prepared for unexpected questions. No matter how well rehearsed a personal reference is, he or she can't have an answer prepared for every basic and probing question a good reference checker will use.

3. Personal references will lead you to the neutrals and the detractors (refer back to Figure 14-2). As we mentioned earlier, this inner circle of personal references can quickly lead you to others who also know the candidate, even to those who don't think that highly of him or her.

128

4. Personal references can provide special information about the candidate. Sometimes there is an important concern about the candidate that needs to be cleared up, such as personal problems, family stability, bad habits, or how well past difficulties have been resolved. For example, if you're getting ready to relocate someone to a new part of the country, you would do well to explore how friends think this will affect the candidate's family situation.

I once performed a reference check for a major company that was getting ready to hire a young woman who had a very high-paying job in San Francisco. She was now willing to go to work in a small city at a much lower salary. Talking with her best friends, I quickly discovered that she was dating a young medical doctor in the new town and fully expected they would be married soon—and wanted to concentrate her full attention on this relationship. With this information in hand, her willingness to move made a lot of sense. I have also frequently been asked to try to determine whether a person still has a chemical-dependency problem, which I find his or her friends to be very frank and open in discussing.

Reaching Out

Reaching out to touch someone isn't easy. I find that only about one in six business calls gets through to the intended party on the first try. Sometimes the most you can accomplish on a phone call is finding out when you will be able to speak to the other person. It should rarely take more than two phone calls to reach anyone, as long as you initiate both calls. When you can't reach the other person the first time, don't ask him to return your call. Instead, find out when he will be available, then volunteer to call back again. People will schedule commitments around your call so they will be available to you. If it takes more than two phone calls to reach someone, you're probably not using the right techniques.

I suggest using what I call the "exact-time" method of contact, which I use with great results. This involves, whenever possible, establishing an exact time to talk, and then calling back at exactly that time. In other words, if I'm calling someone or making a return call, I advise the person of the specific time I will call back. I tell her, or the person who is scheduling calls for her, that I will call at a certain time, emphasizing that when her phone rings at that time it will be me.

You would be surprised how often the person I'm calling is literally sitting by the phone waiting for my call. Indeed, there have been times, when for some unavoidable reason, I wasn't able to make the call. When I called later, I was told in no uncertain terms that I hadn't called when I said I would, and the irritated person sitting by the phone or had altered his or her schedule in anticipation of my call. Believe me, this exact-time method can really save time, and it is much more efficient for you as well as for the person you're calling. Try it for all your calls, business and personal; it will save a lot of time and eliminate the frustrating game of telephone tag.

When you're calling people, you need to make it easy and enjoyable on both yourself and the caller. It's just not courteous having someone you want to speak with chasing you down or playing telephone tag. In fact, unless you make it easy, both of you may just give up.

In my private reference-checking practice, I call all over the country and throughout the world. I have a big map of the United States on the wall of my office in front of my desk. When I call a particular location I mentally travel to that spot on the map. I ask briefly about local happenings and the weather, thereby taking advantage of my brief but important chance to speak with someone who is there. I do the same thing on international calls by swinging around to my back wall which has a world map with time zones. It's my way of traveling every day and enjoying the work I do. I truly believe this makes me a more enjoyable and interested caller.

References by Mail

Assuming the job applicant has a job history, efforts to check the applicant's background by mail may be futile. Previous employers may be slow in answering the queries you solicit through the mail. Or, they may not answer at all. Studies have shown that the return rate can be as high as 56 percent and as low as 35 percent. The reason for the overall low return rate is that many employers are concerned that former employees may take them to court over information written on a reference form.

Another problem is that it takes too long, usually two or three weeks, to receive a reply. If you are trying to hire special categories of applicants who are in short supply, candidates just won't wait for you to go through this long and involved process.

You are far better off checking references by phone. You get more comprehensive information—spending less time and effort—if you follow the telephone practices outlined in this book. However, for the categories of information outlined below, you may have to use the mail.

Searching Public Records

A publication is available entitled, *The Guide to Background Investigations,* which provides addresses, phone numbers, and procedures necessary for accessing public records. This 700-page reference manual details all the information needed to conduct a search of the nation's public records by mail, phone or fax, including:

1. CRIMINAL RECORDS—procedures for each of the nation's 3,178 county courthouses and state repositories are described. Simple, complete instructions for conducting criminal record searches by phone or mail are included. Over 1,500 counties will do free searches by phone for employers.

2. WORKERS' COMPENSATION RECORDS—check job-related injuries and claims. *The Guide* reveals the procedures used in all 50 states for releasing workers' compensation records for employment purposes.

3. DRIVING RECORDS—verify legal name, date of birth, and more with motor vehicle reports (MVRs). *The Guide* lists every department of motor vehicles (DMV) in the U.S. and shows how to access their surprisingly valuable records.

4. EDUCATIONAL RECORDS—confirm attendance and degree at 3,500 U.S. colleges and universities. Telephone numbers direct to the registrar's office and school-by-school instructions show what is required.

5. FEDERAL COURT RECORDS—*The Guide* shows how to obtain federal criminal conviction data, civil litigation records, and bankruptcy filings and dispositions from the nation's 93 Federal District Courts. Also included are instructions for each of the 11 Federal Record Centers.

The Guide is easy to use. A city-county cross reference shows which counties control records for over 30,000 municipalities in the U.S. Subdirectories for state, federal, and educational records group similar sources together in logical, alphabetical order. Throughout, you'll receive concise, clear directions on how to obtain individual records.

The Guide to Background Investigations is available from:

> National Employment Screening Services
> 8801 South Yale Avenue
> Tulsa, OK 74137
> (918) 491-9936
> (800)-247-8713
> Fax (918) 491-9946

If you're not satisfied, return it to them within 30 days and nothing is owed.☑

15
POWER CHECKLISTS & QUESTIONS

To gather information, you have to ask the right question, worded the right way, at the right time.

octors use questions to diagnosis diseases; detectives use them to solve crimes; lawyers use them to defend clients; teachers use them to educate children; scientists use them to make new discoveries. Questions are the workhorses of the mind. Without them, mankind's progress would come to a halt.

We have all heard the expression, "If you don't know where you're going, you'll probably end up somewhere else." There's no greater truism when gathering information. If it's not crystal clear in your mind what you want to learn, you probably won't learn it. You can't just "shoot the bull" with someone and then wonder why you didn't get any meaningful information.

The right questions represent more than half the solution to gathering reference information. Asking the right questions dramatically increases the information received. Every question asked during a reference call makes a statement about how good you are at gathering background information. The quality of your questions ultimately will determine the quality of your answers. The questioner is always in control. A common misconception is that the dominant party in a dialogue is the one doing the most talking. Actually, the opposite is true.

One of the major problems most companies have in gathering outside reference information is their telephone questionnaire forms. In most instances, these forms are simple checklists that are used for all reference contact calls—business, personal, and customer. Plus, such forms usually contain a lot of questions with narrow lines for writing in the answers, requiring the reference checker to fill in the blanks. These forms are basically stressful to use.

Before we proceed into what I have found to be a more useful and less stressful way to ask for and record reference information, it's probably best to review the legal compliance aspects of checking references.

1. Be sure you have the candidate's written authorization to verify his or her personal and employment history and other related matters needed in arriving at an employment decision. This normally is included as part of the sign-off on the application for employment or the special form we reviewed earlier in the book.

2. Follow the checklist exactly to obtain the necessary information and opinions. Obviously, each call will be somewhat different, but you should proceed in a preplanned sequence for consistency and thoroughness.

3. For equal opportunity employment compliance, be totally consistent. That is, ask all references the same questions, and never ask different questions of different groups (women, minority members, handicapped, etc.).

4. Report exactly what the reference said: Do not try to interpret the message. If necessary, dig deeper or contact other people for the exact meaning of what was said.

Checklists

At the end of this chapter, you will find some sample checklists to help guide you in calling references (Figure 15-1 through 15-4). There is a separate sheet for each type of reference contact—business, personal, customer, and one for contacting someone about hourly employees. They have to be different for each type of contact because the flow of questions is different. When disrupted from the logical pattern of questioning for a particular type of reference, the reference checker loses credibility and has more difficulty doing the job. The questions in the sample forms at the end of this chapter were predesigned for the type of reference being contacted.

Also, notice that these reference-calling forms are laid out differently from the ones used by most companies. In these, the questions are on the left hand side; the right side serves as a work space. When information is coming in fast, it is necessary to be able to write freely, to draw arrows connecting related information, or to circle important facts. It's a lot easier and more natural than trying to fill blank spaces on a tightly printed form. In one of my seminars, a lady pointed out that this made a lot of sense to her. She used a yellow pad next to her company reference-checking form to give her plenty of room to write. She then rewrote the information onto her checklist when she had time. In my opinion, this method is just too inefficient and time consuming.

When calling references, the flow of questions must be right. For this reason, the placement and wording of the questions in my sample calling forms has been tested and retested to maximize their effectiveness. For example, the checklists start with simple verification questions, then move to performance-related information, then to developmental opinions, and finally to networking your reference contacts. I have tried as much as possible to use indirect questions— that is, questions that get the desired information without requiring the reference to give a personal opinion or explanation. Note that there is a space in each question to use the applicant's (first) name.

Let's look at what I consider to be key questions on the *Business Reference* checklist (Figure 15-1), and how I have found them useful.

Question No. 9: *Is (John) honest?*

I ask it just this way. The reference will immediately reply affirmatively, or will hesitate and start groping for an answer—in which case I push to learn why he or she is having difficulty giving a clear reply.

Question No. 10: *Have you seen (John's) current résumé?*

Let me read what it says were his duties and accomplishments with your organization.

If you remember nothing else from this book, remember this technique. If you suspect that the candidate's résumé is inflated or wrong, read it to the reference. I can't tell you how many times this has worked for me and other people who use it. If there is an error or lie on the résumé, the reference will tip you off by his or her reaction, sometimes even laughing at how out of line it is. And, the person will tell you what it should be. You can also use this when someone just will not participate in giving you reference information. Ask if you can at least read to them what (John) said on his résumé. Usually, the reference contact will agree and then will make valuable comments about what's stated on the résumé.

Question No. 12: *How did (John's) last job performance review go?*

What strengths were cited? What recommended improvement areas were noted? How about the performance review prior to the last one?

Why try to reinvent the wheel? If you're talking to the applicant's previous supervisor, rather than ask for an opinion about the candidate, why not have him or her relay what was reported on the last performance review? It doesn't require any new judgment or opinion, so there should be much less resistance in providing the information. Ask if the employee was given a copy of the performance report. If so, you may want to have him bring it in for your personal review.

Question No. 17: *What is the biggest change you've observed in (John)? Where has there been the most growth?*

I can tell when the reference doesn't want to tell me something unfavorable about the candidate. However, I know this question will help uncover the information. The reason is that the reference will try to help the applicant by explaining how he has made a great improvement in the area he is weakest in.

The *Personal Reference* checklist (Figure 15-2) is for use with someone who knows the candidate only on a personal basis, but has not worked with him. It is self-explanatory and appropriate for this type of relationship.

Figure 15-3, the *Customer Reference* checklist, is for contacting someone on whom a sales applicant has called. The questions fit this type of business relationship, and will produce very valuable information.

The *Hourly Employee Reference* checklist (Figure 15-4) is designed for reference contacts on hourly employees. I developed it for a major corporation to get quick and meaningful information to ensure that no mistakes were made when hiring someone to work in the company's plants. Once you've established contact with the reference, it takes only about five or ten minutes to get this basic information.

Some Tips

If the reference you call just won't cooperate in any way, there is one last fallback technique that can make the call worthwhile. Describe the new company and the job the candidate will be performing. Ask the reference for his opinion as to whether this position will be right for the applicant. You will be surprised how often the person will give you his view on this question. Then, at least, your time has been productive rather than wasted.

Always start your reference checking with education. I've found that about one out of twelve job candidates inflates or falsifies his or her educational qualifications. With few exceptions, you can verify school attendance and degrees attained over the phone. Call your own school to see how easy it is to get this information. If you find a discrepancy in education, you may not want to proceed any further. If you do, you'll already be alert to the possibility of fraud.

Look for extremes and their opposite condition. For example, the biggest flaw that many aggressive people have is that they may take on more tasks than they can handle and end up dropping the ball on many of them. Or, they may not be sensitive to the needs of others. Another example would be workaholics, many of whom have not learned how to delegate properly. Any time you have an overwhelming strength, turn the coin over and see what you have. In all of us, our biggest strength is normally also our biggest weakness.

With rapidly rising medical costs confronting companies, an interest in potential employees' health seems to have a sound business basis. Whether they admit it or not, general health is on the minds of most personnel officers, especially in small- and medium-sized companies. Many try to determine a candidate's health level by asking about exercise habits, smoking, and drinking. Many also give drug tests. The candidate's fitness and health have become major criteria of employability, although this is not easy to measure, and a substantial number of companies will not be likely hire someone in poor health.

Accuracy of Information

I once had a reference ask me to read back what I had picked up from what he said to me. I had no objection and did so. He listened and commented that my interpretation was correct and in fact complimented me on my good listening and thoroughness. This has happened to me on only one occasion in over 30 years of making reference calls. You would think that more references would want to be sure that what they have explained and commented on is, in fact, being understood and recorded properly by the reference checker. Again, we seemed to have lost a lot of our common sense in the area of exchanging and explaining background information.☑

Figure 15-1

Business Reference

Candidate	Person Contacted
Potential position:	Position _____
Job _____	Company _____
Company _____	Location _____
	Business Tel. _____
	Home Tel. _____

Question   *Response*

Verification

1. I'd like to verify _____ 's dates of employment from _____ to _____ .

2. What type of work did _____ do? (Title/general duties)

3. Were __ 's earnings $ _____ per _____? Were there any bonus or incentive plans?

4. Why did _____ leave the company?

Performance

5. Did _____ supervise other people? How many? How effectively?

6. What are _____ 's strong points on the job? What characteristics do you most admire about him/her?

Question	*Response*

7. How would you rate _____ 's job performance on a scale of 1 to 10 (10 being high) compared to other people you have observed who are in a similar capacity?

8. What does _____ do when s/he has a complaint or something doesn't go well? How does s/he handle stress?

9. Is _____ honest?

10. Have you seen _____ 's current résumé? Let me read you what it says were the duties and accomplishments with your organization. (Stop at each significant point, and as the reference for a comment.)

11. How well does _____ relate to other people? Which employees does s/he work best with:
❑ superiors ❑ peers
❑ subordinates?

12. How did _____ 's last job performance review go? What strengths were cited? What recommended improvement areas were noted? How about the performance review prior to the last one?

13. On the average, how many times a month does _____ miss work or come in late? Does s/he have any personal problems, illness, or bad habits that interfere with job performance?

14. When you heard _____ was leaving, was a counter offer or effort made to try to keep him/her?

Question	*Response*

*15. Who did _____ work for prior to
   joining your company?*

*16. When _____ was hired, were his/her
   references checked? Who checked these
   references? And, what did the references
   have to say?*

Developmental

*17. What is the biggest change you've
   observed in _____? Where has there
   been the most growth?*

*18. Is _____ in the right job/career?
   How far can s/he go?*

*19. If _____ asked you what one thing
   would most improve the way s/he performs
   on the job, what advice would you give?*

*20. What is the best way to work with
   _____ to quickly maximize his/her
   talents and effectiveness for the company?*

Networking

21. What other person(s) know _____?

Name: _____	*Name:* _____
Title: _____	*Title:* _____
Location: _____	*Location:* _____
Tel: _____	*Tel:* _____

Overall Rating:
❑ *Excellent*   ❑ *Good*   ❑ *Some Reservation*   ❑ *Poor*

Check made by _____ *Date* _____
Comments/summary: _____

Source: Certified Reference Checking Company

Figure 15-2

Personal Reference

Candidate

Potential position:
Job _____
Company _____

Person Contacted

Position _____
Company _____
Location _____
Business Tel. _____
Home Tel. _____

Question   *Response*

Verification

1. *How long have you known* _____ *?*
   What is his/her relationship to you?

2. *How often do you see (or talk to)*
   _____ *?*

Performance

3. *What is your opinion of* _____ *'s*
   character, dependability, and
   general reputation?

4. *What would you say are* _____ *'s*
   strong points?

5. *What specific personal trait or skill*
   is _____ *trying to improve on?*

6. *What basic values does* _____
   hold for himself/herself?

142

Question	*Response*

7. How is _____ health?
   Does s/he have any personal
   problems or bad habits that you
   have ever noticed?

8. Is _____ honest?
   Can you give an example?

Developmental

9. What is the biggest change you've
   observed in _____?
   Where has s/he grown the most?

Networking

10. What other person(s) know_____?

Name: _____   Name: _____
Title: _____   Title: _____
Location: _____   Location: _____
Tel: _____   Tel: _____

Name: _____   Name: _____
Title: _____   Title: _____
Location: _____   Location: _____
Tel: _____   Tel: _____

Name: _____   Name: _____
Title: _____   Title: _____
Location: _____   Location: _____
Tel: _____   Tel: _____

Overall Rating:
❏ *Excellent*   ❏ *Good*   ❏ *Some Reservation*   ❏ *Poor*

Check made by _____ *Date* _____
Comments/summary:

Source: Certified Reference Checking Company

Figure 15-3

Customer Reference

Candidate	*Person Contacted*
Potential position:	Position _____
Job _____	Company _____
Company _____	Location _____
	Business Tel. _____
	Home Tel. _____

Question	*Response*

Verification

1. How long did _____ call on you? Did s/he open your account?

2. How often did _____ call on you?

3. When _____ was calling on you, did you purchase less, more, or about the same amount?

Performance

4. How would you rank _____ performance compared with other sales people who call on you: ❏ top 10% ❏ top 25% ❏ top 50%.

5. Were you satisfied with the way _____ serviced your account?

6. Was there anything that _____ did, or did not do, that pleased you? . . . or displeased you?

Question	*Response*

7. Did _____ keep you abreast of
   what was happening in the industry?

8. If _____ were to again be calling on
   you with another company, would
   you be ❏ pleased ❏ displeased
   ❏ neutral?

Developmental

9. What is the biggest change you've
   observed in _____?
   Where has s/he grown the most?

10. What other person(s) know _____?

Name: _____   Name: _____
Title: _____   Title: _____
Location: _____   Location: _____
Tel: _____   Tel: _____

Name: _____   Name: _____
Title: _____   Title: _____
Location: _____   Location: _____
Tel: _____   Tel: _____

Name: _____   Name: _____
Title: _____   Title: _____
Location: _____   Location: _____
Tel: _____   Tel: _____

Overall Rating:
❏ *Excellent*   ❏ *Good*   ❏ *Some Reservation*   ❏ *Poor*

Check made by _____ *Date* _____
Comments/summary:

Source: Certified Reference Checking Company

Figure 15-4

Hourly Employee—Reference Check

_____	_____
Candidate	*Person Contacted*

Potential position:
Job _____
Company _____

Position _____
Company _____
Location _____
Business Tel. _____
Home Tel. _____

1. _____ *said s/he worked for you from* _____ *to* _____ *as a* _____ .
   Is this correct? ❑ *Yes* ❑ *No*

2. *How often did you observe* _____ *on the job?*

3. *How was* _____ *'s attitude? Did she fit in with the other workers?*

4. *Was* _____ *'s attendance OK? How often was s/he late or absent?*

5. *Was* _____ *honest?* ❑ *Yes* ❑ *No Any evidence to the contrary?*

6. *Does* _____ *have any personal problems, sickness, or bad habits that interfere with job performance?* ❑ *Yes* ❑ *No*
   Did s/he ever have any work accidents? ❑ *Yes* ❑ *No*

7. *What were* _____ *'s strong points?*   *Weak points?*

8. *How productive was* _____ *? How are his/her quality standards?*

9. *How much supervision does* _____ *require? How fast does s/he learn?*

10. *Why did* _____ *leave? Would you rehire him/her?* ❑ *Yes* ❑ *No*

Overall Rating:
❑ *Excellent*   ❑ *Good*   ❑ *Some Reservation*   ❑ *Poor*

Check made by _____ *Date* _____
Comments/summary:

Source: Certified Reference Checking Company

THE REJECTED APPLICANT

Whatever you do, treat the rejected applicant with respect and dignity. And, always protect your sources of information.

I believe that employment rejection is a special and very misunderstood subject that needs to be examined. In my many years in the employment business, I have seen more confusion on how to handle the case of the rejected applicant than on any other aspect of the employment process.

All too often, we don't want to hurt the job applicant's feelings, so we try to "sugar coat" the rejection in the hope that we both will feel better about the whole situation. However, with this new system of having the candidate contact and set up the reference calls, it may be very obvious why you rejected the applicant after you have spoken with his or her references. The applicant will surmise that he or she apparently did not "make it" because of what the references said, and may even want to know what was said and by whom.

When speaking with a reference, always reassure him that what he says will be treated as confidential information. You have an obligation to keep this information under virtual lock and key, never letting the applicant know what was said.

Before we look at the rejected finalist, let's look at another problem that also needs addressing—how to advise candidates that, after the interview, they are no longer contenders for the job opening. Many interviewers will tell everyone they are in the running and keep all the candidates up in the air. The problem with this nice-guy technique (which is a form of avoidance) is that some applicants will take this to mean they are viable candidates, falsely get their hopes up, and sometimes even quit interviewing with other employers. To avoid this, I suggest you advise the candidate in whom you no longer have an interest along these lines: "You are a *fine candidate* and we appreciate you taking the time to talk with us. However, we will also be talking with other qualified people, and you *should continue* your interviewing activity." Above all, always let the applicant leave the interview feeling positive about your company. Looking for a job is never easy, so make the visit with you as painless and pleasant as possible.

Now for the applicant who knows he or she was a finalist, but for whatever reason—sometimes bad references—doesn't get the job. *Never* divulge or try to explain the factors that went into your decision, because you probably don't know all of them yourself. Above all, *never* tell the candidate that your decision was the result of derogatory information received from references. This is just dangerous and unnecessary. Do yourself and the candidate a favor: (*a*) Get on with your business, and (*b*) let the candidate get on with his or her life. I suggest you advise the finalist in whom you no longer have no interest along these lines: "It was *very, very* close, and certainly a difficult decision for us to make, . . . but we have decided on another candidate that *we feel* most closely meets our needs *at this time.*"

File your reference notes and reports separately. A personnel record should not include employee references supplied to an employer if the identity of the person making the reference would be disclosed. In fact, I recommend destroying all your reference notes after you have made your hiring decision.

Believe me, if you have ever violated these rules, as I have on occasion during my career, and told someone in pretty specific terms why he or she didn't get the job—thinking I was being helpful—you would think twice about ever going beyond what I recommend. If you don't follow my simple advice, you will literally spend weeks defending yourself, your company, and even your references from the complex inquisition of a rejected job candidate. When it's all over, no one has gained from it—especially the candidate.

My favorite story in this regard came from a participant at one of my seminars on reference checking. A job candidate asked why he didn't get the job after everything and everybody seemed to be going his way—as far as he could tell. He was told by the employment manager that everyone liked him except the president of the company, who was not impressed and told them not to hire him. After hearing this, the candidate immediately insisted on seeing the president, causing much disruption and embarrassment to the president. As a result of this poor handling of the employment rejection, both the vice president of human resources and the employment manager were terminated by the company within the next three months. ☑

IT COMES OUT THIS WAY

*What we know . . . but don't see about
how to relate to reference contacts.*

❑ People basically want to help another person get a new job.

❑ Most people will be totally honest about someone they know or have worked with.

❑ It is up to us to ask the right questions in order to get correct and insightful information about someone we may hire.

❑ We have to recognize the personal needs and concerns of each reference in order to get full cooperation and honesty in providing us with the information we want.

❑ To really find out what we want, we have to be politely persistent and skillful in making reference contacts.

And in conclusion . . .

❑　In view of these considerations, it is our responsibility as reference checkers to use the right techniques and questions to get the information we need to make a smart hiring decision.

CONCLUSION

It's time we do a better job of identifying and weeding out undesirable job candidates. We owe that to our organizations.

At the beginning of this book, I gave you my background-checking formula. You've probably forgotten it by now, so let's look at it again:

$$7W(LL) + IC + RT = SHD$$

Now you're ready for the translation: *Seven ways* a candidate can deceive you multiplied by the *legal limits* you must stay within, plus *involving the candidate* and using the *right techniques* equals a *smart hiring decision.* If you apply the effort on the left, you can't miss getting the results on the right.

In this book I've described some of the things I've learned in almost 30 years of hiring people. I have tried to bring some useful insights to the subject of screening applicants. Times have changed and job candidates just aren't as honest as they used to be. It's time for applied creativity—that is, creativity that "rolls up its sleeves and gets to work." Creativity helps provide "quantum leaps" in improving the hiring process, a process that hasn't changed much over the years. Used properly, the creative techniques described in these pages can produce real gains for employers trying to hire the right people.

I'm sure you will agree by now that it is more important than ever to check candidates' references. It is necessary and proper to validate through others what candidates believe or say about themselves. Only by talking in-depth to those individuals who have been closely associated with the candidates is a true evaluation possible. Background information about candidates is necessary for a smart hiring decision.

The recruitment process can be long and time consuming, depending on the level of the opening to be filled. In a typical recruiting effort, about 25 percent of the time is spent searching for candidates; 28 percent, screening replies and résumés; 37 percent, interviewing; at least 10 percent should be spent checking references. That's a full hiring sequence, and making it a winning sequence requires both application and creativity.

Networking

I can't emphasize enough the value of networking when checking out job candidates. A large company with which I am familiar hired a top-level research executive who was given an elaborate employment contract, costly relocation provisions, and other expensive benefits. After being on the new job a short time, it was obvious he was not working out. He had severe personality problems and clearly was in over his head professionally. He was obviously a poor choice, and everyone wondered how he could have been hired. Finally, the chairman of the new company called his counterpart, the chairman of the man's former company. He was quickly told that the individual had been slipping badly for several years, quite noticeably in the past few months, and, in fact, was about to be terminated when the new company hired him. The chairman at the former employer went on to say, ". . . we couldn't believe it when we heard you were hiring him," adding, "we were glad to see it because you solved a big problem for us and saved us a lot of money." He went on to tell the chairman of the new company that he would have been glad to tell someone in the proper position what was going on, but was never contacted. Well, the company chairman called in the appropriate staff members and told them the story, wanting to know why no effort had been made to contact the former employer. To make a long story short, the vice president of human resources was reprimanded and shortly thereafter resigned, and the director of professional staffing was fired. There just was no excuse for making an important and costly company decision without doing the necessary background review.

More and more companies are networking with each other regarding the hiring of people. Why fly by the seat of your pants when there is someone like yourself that you can contact at another employer? I guarantee, in most cases, even though you have never met the references with whom you are speaking, they will tell you everything you want to know about someone you are about to hire. If you're not networking to learn the past background of potential employees, you are missing the boat.

A special word for human resource types. You're not simply managing the personnel function of your company, you're influencing your company's future. Everyone of you has a counterpart at every company for which a job applicant has ever worked. Why not call that individual and ask for information, perhaps off the record, about the candidate? It will work in the vast majority of cases. Yet very few ever do this. It's time for the human resource function to be more bold and results-oriented—instead of trying to invent reasons or procedures to keep something from working.

One of the reasons I wrote this book is that the human resource specialty has "botched" this subject so badly, a whole new body of knowledge has developed. In my view, they (human resource specialists) would have done a far greater service had they figured out sensible ways to exchange job performance data about current or past employees— avoiding the need to have to devise ingenious ways to get this information.

The personnel function has undergone a dramatic change in the past 15 years, evolving from an administrative (almost clerical) job to one of the most important areas of business. A company's employees represent its largest expense line item (with the largest and most regular cash flow outlay), and its greatest asset. Decisions in human resources can have a very positive or negative effect on the company's success.

As we approach the twenty-first century, we must rethink the entire hiring process. This will mean exploring new alternatives. It's time for human resource professionals to do everything legal and possible to ensure they are hiring the right people. To stay on the leading edge—to become proactive, not reactive—about tracking a person's work history is a must in today's complex and confusing world.

Does It Pay Off?

A company with which I am familiar started checking references on all job candidates before hiring them. It kept records for a full year, before and after checking references, with the following results:

	Control Year	2nd Year*
Number of candidates interviewed	168	153
Number finalists	44	38
Number of reference checks completed	0	38
Number hired	29	22
Number hired who were hired and then left the company	16	2

*with reference checks

Did this pay off? You bet it did! The bottom line was that the company had a much higher calibre work force and a greatly reduced turnover. It also had better production figures, less friction among employees, and, in the long run, had to spend far less time hiring new people.

Reference checking becomes self-perpetuating because your own employees will refer their friends to your company. Good people know other good people, just like bad people know other bad people; hiring more good people will make your company a winner.

Turnover Has Many Costs

Turnover has both dollar and psychic costs to a company as shown below:

Turnover Cost

Dollars	*Psychic*
Recruitment (ads, agencies, etc.)	Lower morale
Interviewing time	Disruption in workplace
Wasted salary	Personal stress to supervisor/peer/employee
Wasted training/time	Personal stress to supervisor/peer/employee
Lost business	Lost productivity

Which Results In

Up to $15k spent on non-exempt employees	Cannot be measured but is definitely a key factor
Up to $75k spent on exempt employees	

Common Sense and Winning the Hiring Game

A lot of making hiring decisions is common sense, and common sense should rule at every company. Hiring the right people is good business because good people do good work, while bad people do lousy work. Getting good new people is critical, but it also reminds the ones who are already with the company that they are important. Let them know that they're special if they work for your company. You're not just filling slots, you're looking for capable, caring, conscientious people—and you're going to be sure they are this way before you hire them. Getting hired by your company generates pride for the new employee and the entire work force.

Sometimes I think we have lost sight of the practical side of hiring people. There really is no substitute for common sense when picking the right person for your organization, and I suspect most executives would agree with me. Is checking the background of a candidate a good investment? Imagine the trouble it takes to fire someone who doesn't work out. This makes the up-front investment look quite smart. Let the good ones come to work for you, and let the bad ones work for your competitor! You can win the hiring game by using common sense, and by creatively using the effective background screening techniques outlined in this book. ☑

APPENDIX

The following pages contain actual reference reports sent to major companies. Obviously, the names of people and companies have been changed to protect confidentiality.

The long report is used when a client needs to review exactly what was said by each reference. It is appropriate when there are complicated circumstances or when serious/negative observations have been made about the job candidate, which the client should hear and analyze.

The short or summary report saves time in preparing and reading, and is appropriate when information received about the applicant is very positive and consistent, and a detailed elaboration of what was said by each reference is not necessary or needed.

Reference Report   (SAMPLE)
Summary

TO: Big Mountain Mining Corporation
Route 109
Boulder, Colorado

ATTENTION: Ms. Carol J. Hyster

CANDIDATE: Mr. Alan W. Copeland

REFERENCE REPORT

Between September 4 to 8, 1991, I spoke with the following people regarding Mr. Copeland. These parties were told the information they provided would be treated confidentially. The references contacted and their general observations and comments were as follows:

PROFESSIONAL

1.   Mr. Kenneth Lowry, Manager Technologies, Central West Mining Corporation, Denver, Colorado

    Mr. Lowry has known Mr. Copeland for the past 12 years since they worked together at Consolidated Zinc Company. He was the plant manager and Copeland's direct supervisor for approximately 6 years.

    He said that Copeland is certainly an individual with strong technical and management abilities "who is able to get a lot out of his people." Copeland supervised up to 120 employees at the company and, in his opinion, was a highly effective leader and supervisor. He said Copeland is excellent in working with people and described this as probably his strongest management strength. Overall he would rate Copeland as a 7-8 on a scale of 10 (10 being high) compared to other production managers within the company.

    He pointed out that Copeland is "a very serious minded person" who is willing to work hard and tries to accomplish a lot in his job. If he had any criticism, it would be that Copeland sometimes tends to take on too many duties and responsibilities which places him under a great amount of work pressure. However, he did point out that Copeland is able to handle heavy workloads and pressure very well. He said that "Copeland is a person who is as honest as the day is long," and does not have any serious personal problems, sickness or bad habits that ever interfered with his job performance.

CERTIFIED REFERENCE CHECKING
COMPANY
3466 Bridgeland Dr. • Suite 203 • Bridgeton, Missouri 63044 • (314) 739-6787 • FAX (314) 291-8595

He explained that over the years Copeland has become more competent in his field. He believes supervision is Copeland's strongest suit, and is where he should be assigned. If he had any recommendation for Copeland, it would be to possibly pace himself a little better in order to not be overwhelmed by the work he wants to accomplish. He felt the best way to work with Copeland is to support him in every way, pointing out that Copeland likes some feedback regarding his progress.

He explained that Copeland is now assigned at their Warren, Montana location under a plant manager who is considered to be an extremely difficult person to work for. He is aware from conversations with Copeland that Copeland has had enough of the situation and is actively pursuing other employment opportunities, commenting that he does not blame him for doing so.

2. Mr. James Murphy, Senior Metallurgist, Central West Mining Corporation, Denver, Colorado

Mr. Murphy has known Mr. Copeland since they worked together at Consolidated Zinc from 1979 through 1984. He reported to Copeland for about a one year period during that time.

He said "Copeland certainly has good skills" and is a very effective supervisor for the company. Copeland works hard, solves problems and has a reputation for getting the job done. He also commented that Copeland is a very safety minded manager. He explained that Copeland has had responsibility for anywhere from 12 to 50 people with the company and is considered to be an effective leader, explaining that Copeland is a friendly person who gets along well with everyone at all levels.

In his view, Copeland is a very dedicated and self motivated individual who always tries to do his very best. He commented that Copeland is not as technically strong as some other management members who have an engineering degree but Copeland certainly has a sound technical understanding. If he had any comment about Copeland it would be that Copeland could be a little bit more forceful at times. In his opinion Copeland is an honest individual with strong personal principles who is always on the job putting in more time than is required.

Over the years he has watched Copeland improve his technical ability and people skills. He feels Copeland is probably a better production manager than an engineering staff member. If he had any recommendation for Copeland it would be to strengthen his technical background, commenting that he knows Copeland has done this, plus Copeland has become quite

CERTIFIED REFERENCE CHECKING
COMPANY

3466 Bridgeland Dr. • Suite 203 • Bridgeton, Missouri 63044 • (314) 739-6787 • FAX (314) 291-8595

knowledgeable in computerization. In his opinion, the best way to work with Copeland is to spell out his role clearly and then let him alone to do the job. He does feel Copeland likes recognition for the job he is doing and works best when this is given to him. Without question he would recommend Copeland to a new employer.

He knows Copeland is not happy working for his current boss at the Warren, Montana location, explaining that he does not blame Copeland for wanting to make a change at this time in his career.

3. <u>Mr. John March, Supv. of Human Relations and Safety, Warren Refining Co., Warren, Montana</u>

Mr. March and Mr. Copeland have been co-workers at the plant since 1989.

He explained that Copeland is a hardworking and results oriented supervisor. Copeland, who has been responsible for 50 or more hourly employees, has been consistently recognized and promoted within the company. He said Copeland works especially well with other people both in a union and non-union environment.

He commented that Copeland is a dedicated manager who always wants to do his very best. Copeland listens well, is very flexible and can handle varied and complex situations in a plant. He believes that without question Copeland is very honest and reliable, pointing out that Copeland is always early and is usually one of the last to leave. He does not believe Copeland has any personal problems that have ever interfered with his job performance.

He feels production supervision is the right field for Copeland and that Copeland very much enjoys being in charge of people. He felt the best way to work with Copeland is to clearly define his work and responsibilities and then let him alone to get the job done. He does feel that Copeland functions best when given some feedback regarding his progress on the job. Without question, he would recommend Copeland to a new employer.

He is very familiar with Copeland's current situation at the plant and understand his desire to make a job change at this time. He explained that Copeland as well as many other people at the plant basically do not get along with the current plant manager. It has become a difficult situation for Copeland and as a result, it would be best for Copeland to find a new career position. He firmly believes Copeland will be a valuable manager for a new employer.

CERTIFIED REFERENCE CHECKING
COMPANY

3466 Bridgeland Dr. • Suite 203 • Bridgeton, Missouri 63044 • (314) 739-6787 • FAX (314) 291-8595

4. <u>Mr. Mary Nolte, Senior Clerk, Briggs Copper Company, Tucson,</u>
   <u>Arizona</u>

   Ms. Nolte explained that under company policy, information
   about a past employee can only be provided by written
   request. She was adamant that no information would be given
   about Mr. Copeland or anyone else because it would be a
   violation of their policy.

<u>EDUCATION</u>

5. <u>Ms. Linda Lester, Recorder, University of Texas at Dallas, TX</u>

   Ms. Lester verified that Mr. Copeland received a Bachelor's
   degree in Business Administration with a minor in Metallurgy
   from the university in May, 1974. She is not permitted to
   release information about a student's grades or campus
   activities.

<u>SUMMARY</u>

During the above background review, I verified Mr. Copeland's
work history and attempted to detect any possible problem areas.
Based on these conversations, the following facts and conclusions
can be drawn:

A. Mr. Copeland is considered to be a knowledgeable, hardworking
   and effective production supervisor.

B. He is especially effective at working with other people, in
   fact, this was described as his strongest management
   strength.

C. He does not have an engineering degree and may not have the
   heavy technical background required for some positions in the
   industry.

D. He is a very dedicated, serious minded and self motivated
   individual who is willing to take on a large amount of work.
   A comment was made that he sometimes takes on more than he
   may reasonably be able to handle.

E. All the references agreed that production management is
   something he enjoys and is certainly the right field for him.

F. He is currently employed in a situation where he reports to a
   boss who has a reputation for being difficult to work for.
   As a result, he feels it would be best to find a new career
   position at this time. The persons spoken with who knew of

CERTIFIED REFERENCE CHECKING
COMPANY
3466 Bridgeland Dr. • Suite 203 • Bridgeton, Missouri 63044 • (314) 739-6787 • FAX (314) 291-8595

his current situation agreed that his reason for leaving is
valid and thought he would personally be better off working
for a new employer.

G. All the references thought highly of him as a production
    supervisor in the metals processing industry and do recommend
    him to a new employer.

Compiled by: William P. Lutz   Date: September 12, 1991

CERTIFIED REFERENCE CHECKING
COMPANY

3466 Bridgeland Dr. • Suite 203 • Bridgeton, Missouri 63044 • (314) 739-6787 • FAX (314) 291-8595

Reference Report Summary   (SAMPLE)

TO: Boswell Corporation
1201 South Lackland
Dayton, Ohio 45401

ATTENTION: Mr. Albert W. Johnson

CANDIDATE: Mr. Robert A. Everly

CONFIDENTIAL

REFERENCE REPORT

Between September 9 to 14, 1991, I spoke with the following people regarding Mr. Everly. These parties were told the information they provided would be treated confidentially.

1. Mr. Matthew Woods, OEM Sales Manager, Compra Systems, Inc., Boston, Massachusetts

2. Mr. William Kentwell, Sales Manager, Blake Palmer Company, Latrope, Pennsylvania

3. Dr. James Smith, Dean, Graduate School of Business, New Brighton College, Concord, New Hampshire

4. Mr. Charles Matson, Regional Sales Manager, Parac Industrial Co., Bedford, Massachusetts

5. Ms. Joan Davis, Clerk, Western Michigan State University, Springfield, MI

SUMMARY

During the above background review, I verified Mr. Everly's work history and attempted to detect any possible problem areas. Based on these conversations, the following facts and conclusions can be drawn:

PROFESSIONAL

A. Mr. Everly was described as a very experienced, hardworking and highly competent sales representative. He has consistently ranked at the very top of the sales force with his current employer, normally being either first or second in the standing of their sales representatives.

B. He is considered to be a very self-motivated and self-driven individual who is determined to be successful and will do whatever is necessary to be a top sales performer. He has an excellent sales background and has always performed in an exemplary manner.

CERTIFIED REFERENCE CHECKING
COMPANY

3466 Bridgeland Dr. • Suite 203 • Bridgeton, Missouri 63044 • (314) 739-6787 • FAX (314) 291-8595

C. He is a very thorough individual who does excellent follow-up with his customers. He gains their respect and confidence, which was considered one of the reasons for his high level of success.

D. He was described as a very likeable and personable individual who is able to get along quite well with people at all levels. Although he is aggressive, he does not intimidate or irritate people and is, therefore, able to get their support and commitment.

E. He is a part time college teacher who always receives top ratings from his students. It was noted that he is always helpful and willing to take extra steps to assist students.

PERSONAL

F. He is a very positive, aggressive and determined individual who is fully committed to reach his personal goals.

G. Everyone spoken with felt he is a totally honest and reliable person who can always be counted upon to give his very best effort.

G. Comments were made that if he has any weakness, it would be that he sometimes works too hard and is somewhat of a perfectionist.

H. It was pointed out that he really does want to help people and will literally go out of his way to assist someone because he receives a great amount of personal satisfaction in doing this.

I. He is a very money motivated person who wants to be financially successful. In fact, he is continually exploring new ways to increase his earnings.

J. Everyone commented that he is a good family man. One reference commented that he has two loves in his life, his job and his family.

K. He has never had any serious personal problems, sickness or bad habits that ever interfered with his job performance.

L. It was confirmed he received an M.B.A. degree from Western Michigan State University as stated on his resume.

CERTIFIED REFERENCE CHECKING
COMPANY

3466 Bridgeland Dr. • Suite 203 • Bridgeton, Missouri 63044 • (314) 739-6787 • FAX (314) 291-8595

<u>OVERALL</u>

M. All the references spoken with stated that over the years he has been maturing and growing as a businessman and sales representative. He is continually improving his skills and abilities.

N. There was no question in anyone's mind that selling is the right career for him and that he really loves this activity. A number of comments were made that he is the type of individual who probably does not want and should not be placed into sales management because he seems to thrive and excel as a field sales person.

O. A comment was made that he can be impatient at times, and needs to understand the limits of the management team that support him. Although this was not a serious problem, he does move so fast on his own that sometimes the support he needs has difficulty staying up with him.

P. It was suggested that the best way to work with him is to continually pile on the work and keep adding new responsibilities and goals for him.

Q. A number of the references spoken with commented how he is able to handle a tremendously large volume of work and activity. He is quite community minded and has heavy involvements outside of work. He thrives on activity and success and needs this kind of stimulation in his life.

R. A number of the references spoken with explained that Compra (his current employer) is going through considerable problems and possible downsizing, and he is willing to make a job change because of the great uncertainty in the company, especially if the new job offers more income potential.

S. Comments were made that he is the kind of person who needs a minimum of direction, however, he does like and appreciates management recognition. It seems important to him to be recognized for the high standing he has within his company.

T. He appears to be an exemplary person and strong candidate for account management responsibility. One of the references spoken with commented that he will be a tremendous asset wherever he works, and there is no question that he is an outstanding candidate for a sales position with any employer he chooses to consider.

Prepared by: Joseph T. Wylie   Date: September 16, 1991

CERTIFIED REFERENCE CHECKING
COMPANY

3466 Bridgeland Dr. • Suite 203 • Bridgeton, Missouri 63044 • (314) 739-6787 • FAX (314) 291-8595

CHAPTER NOTES

Chapter 6

1. Robert J. Ringer, *Million Dollar Habits* (New York: Wynwood Press, 1990): 175.

Chapter 7

1. Diane Stanton, *Boardroom Reports,* March 15, 1989, pp. 1-2.

2. Julie Ashworth Glover and G. Roger King, *Personnel Administrator* (July 1989): 52-55.

3. Caleb S. Atwood and James M. Neel, *HR Magazine* (October 1990): 74-75.

4. Commentary by Lois Vander Waerdt, *St. Louis Business Journal,* September 19-25, 1988, p. 5A.

5. Marisa Manley, *INC.* (June 1989): 135-139.

Chapter 11

1. Jennifer J. Laabs, "Dangers of a Hard Sell; Misrepresentation of Jobs Can Lead to Employee Dissatisfaction, Even Lawsuits," *Recruitment Today* (January-February 1991): 18-21.

INDEX

About the Smith Collins Company

THE SMITH COLLINS COMPANY offers speaking and consulting services for industry and government. Seminars and workshops are offered on a contractual basis in a variety of areas, including ethical decision making.

OTHER SMITH COLLINS TITLES of interest to readers of this book are *Tough-Minded Management of Problem Employees: Don't Be a Gutless Nice Guy!* by Gareth S. Gardiner ($10.95) and, *In Pursuit of Ethics: Tough Choices in the World of Work*, by O.C. Ferrell and Gareth S. Gardiner ($12.95).

Our 24-hour order fulfillment and
telemarketing number is
1-800-345-0096